Take-off for Taiwan?

CHATHAM HOUSE PAPERS

An Asia-Pacific Programme Publication
Programme Director: Richard Grant

The Royal Institute of International Affairs, at Chatham House in London, has provided an impartial forum for discussion and debate on current international issues for 75 years. Its resident research fellows, specialized information resources, and range of publications, conferences, and meetings span the fields of international politics, economics, and security. The Institute is independent of government.

Chatham House Papers are short monographs on current policy problems which have been commissioned by the RIIA. In preparing the papers, authors are advised by a study group of experts convened by the RIIA, and publication of a paper indicates that the Institute regards it as an authoritative contribution to the public debate. The Institute does not, however, hold opinions of its own; the views expressed in this publication are the responsibility of the authors.

CHATHAM HOUSE PAPERS

Take-off for Taiwan?

Edited by Peter Ferdinand

THE ROYAL INSTITUTE
OF INTERNATIONAL
AFFAIRS

Pinter
A Cassell Imprint
Wellington House, 125 Strand, London WC2R 0BB, United Kingdom

First published in 1996

British Library Cataloguing in Publication Data
A CIP catalogue record for this book is available from the British Library

ISBN 1-85567-116-6 (Paperback)
    1-85567-115-8 (Hardback)

Typeset by Koinonia Limited
Printed and bound in Great Britain by
Biddles Limited, Guildford and King's Lynn

Contents

Acknowledgments

This book has received financial support from a number of sources, including the Taipei Representative Office in London. The authors would like to acknowledge the many helpful suggestions made by the participants at the various study groups held to discuss initial drafts of chapters. The authors themselves are, of course, responsible for any errors which remain. The editor would particularly like to acknowledge the great patience, assistance and skill of Margaret May and the staff of the Publications Department at Chatham House in preparing the final manuscript.

January 1996   P.F.

Contributors

Peter Ferdinand is Director of the Centre for Studies in Democratisation at the University of Warwick. He was formerly Head of the Asia-Pacific Programme at the Royal Institute of International Affairs. He is the author of *Communist Regimes in Comparative Perspective: The Evolution of the Soviet, Chinese and Yugoslav Models* (Wheatsheaf, 1991) and the editor of *The New Central Asia* (RIIA/Pinter, 1994).

Hermann Halbeisen teaches at the University of Bochum in Germany. He is the author of numerous articles on Taiwan and East Asia generally.

Chiao Chiao Hsieh teaches Chinese and East Asian politics at the University of Frankfurt in Germany. She is the author of *Strategy for Survival: The Foreign Policy and External Relations of the Republic of China on Taiwan, 1949–79* (Sherwood, 1985).

Abbreviations

ADB	Asian Development Bank
AEAR	Association of East Asian Relations
AIT	American Institute in Taiwan
APEC	Asia-Pacific Economic Cooperation
ARATS	Association for Relations Across the Taiwan Straits
ASEAN	Association of Southeast Asian Nations
CC	Central Committee
CCNAA	Coordinating Council for North American Affairs
CSC	Central Standing Committee
CSDP	Chinese Social Democratic Party
CY	Control Yuan
DPP	Democratic Progressive Party
ExY	Examination Yuan
EY	Executive Yuan
FAO	Food and Agriculture Organization
GATT	General Agreement on Tariffs and Trade
HCL	New Tide Faction
IBRD	International Bank for Reconstruction and Development
IDA	International Development Agency
IFC	International Finance Corporation
IGO	International Governmental Organization
IMF	International Monetary Fund
INGO	International Non-governmental Organization
IOC	International Olympic Committee
JY	Judicial Yuan
KMT	Kuomintang

LY	Legislative Yuan
NA	National Assembly
NIE	Newly Industrializing Economies
NP	New Party
NT$	New Taiwan Dollar
PBEC	Pacific Basin Economic Council
PECC	Pacific Economic Cooperation Council
PRC	People's Republic of China
ROC	Republic of China (Taiwan)
ROK	Republic of Korea
SEF	Straits Exchange Foundation
TPKMCT	Taiwan, Penghu, Kinmen and Matsu Customs Territory
TRA	Taiwan Relations Act
WHO	World Health Organization
WTO	World Trade Organization

A note on names

The Republic of China on Taiwan officially uses the Wade-Giles system to transliterate names from Chinese, and the People's Republic uses the pinyin system. Therefore in general this book uses Wade-Giles for names from or associated with Taiwan, and the pinyin system for names from or associated with the PRC. This should make it easier for general readers to recognize names used elsewhere. As a compromise, the capital of the mainland is referred to as Peking.

Map of Taiwan

Chapter 1

Introduction

Peter Ferdinand

In the 1950s the Taiwan Straits were one of the potential flashpoints in the confrontation between the West and the communist world. Two crises, in 1955 and 1958, led to artillery duels between the mainland and the offshore islands of Quemoy and Matsu, which were occupied by the Nationalists. The world held its breath, fearing nuclear conflict. After that the area dropped from popular consciousness and media attention.

In the 1990s, however, it has again become a potential flashpoint, as debate on Taiwan over the issue of independence infuriates the People's Republic of China (PRC). In the summer of 1995 the PRC launched a 'test' firing of missiles in the direction of Taiwan. Both sides are rearming their air forces and navies. Although there is no longer any danger of a clash leading to global nuclear conflict, any confrontation would necessarily disrupt shipping through the Straits, damaging international trade. The shares of the ever-growing number of companies around the world with significant investments on either Taiwan or the mainland would dive immediately. Though other states would wish to remain neutral in any confrontation, they could not remain unaffected, and they would come under extreme pressure to take sides. That would particularly affect arms suppliers, principally the United States, France and Russia – all, like the PRC, permanent members of the UN Security Council. Any conflict, therefore, would have repercussions around the world.

Ironically the Republic of China on Taiwan (ROC) probably owes its survival in the 1950s to the late President Kim Il Sung of North Korea. When the communists overran the mainland in 1949, the remnants of the Nationalist forces were forced to retreat to Taiwan. The communists then prepared for an assault across the Taiwan Straits. In late 1949 they

1

launched an attack on Quemoy but were repulsed. Nevertheless, even though Taiwan is a hundred miles offshore and the People's Republic had virtually no navy at that time, the balance of military forces was heavily in the communists' favour. The People's Liberation Army began to prepare for a full-scale assault on Taiwan in 1950. The long-term prospects for the Nationalists were not bright.

In January 1950 US Secretary of State Dean Acheson told the National Press Club that the USA would defend a strategic perimeter from the Aleutian Islands, through Japan and the Ryukyu Islands, down to the Philippines. Neither Taiwan nor South Korea was included, and US embassies around the world were told to prepare themselves for the fall of Taiwan.

On 25 June 1950, however, North Korea made a surprise invasion of the South. Almost immediately President Truman declared that the US Navy would resume patrols in the Taiwan Straits, and a policy of containment was introduced for China as it had been for the Soviet Union. In 1954 the USA signed a Mutual Defence Pact with Taiwan and, until 1979, when it fully recognized the People's Republic as the government of China and withdrew from the Pact, the United States prevented any attack upon Taiwan. During and after the Taiwan Straits crises of 1955 and 1958, the two Chinas were restrained by their respective superpower patrons from taking extreme action.

From these inauspicious beginnings Taiwan has prospered. Despite being forced to withdraw from the United Nations in 1971 and becoming more or less a diplomatic pariah after 1979, it now has the fourth highest per capita GNP in East Asia and is the twelfth largest trading nation. It has managed to preserve a high degree of income equality and has an increasingly sophisticated middle-class consumer market. It has 'taken off' economically.

Researchers in other parts of the world are now attempting to draw lessons from Taiwan's economic success. Business people seek increasingly lucrative deals there. Ministers and officials of foreign governments press for improved access for their exporters and seek to attract investment. Officially Taiwan is little recognized, but unofficially it is much courted.

Since the late 1980s, Taiwan has also rapidly become one of the most developed democracies in East Asia, certainly in the Chinese-speaking world. Although this dimension of its evolution is less well known in other parts of the globe, it deserves to be as widely publicized as its economic success. The Republic of China was always in favour of democracy, but in the future. Now it has a functioning party system with free elections.

One consequence of this upsurge of democracy has been growing debate over Taiwan's international status and identity. The main opposition party, the Democratic Progressive Party (DPP), has made this one of its chief election issues. Many in the party want Taiwan to declare independence from the rest of China. They want a government which pays more attention to the concerns of the people of Taiwan than to reunification. And they want to develop their economy out of the shadow of the mainland. As the proportion of the Taiwanese population with a personal memory of life on the mainland wanes, so too does its emotional attachment to the mainland. On the other hand, most people on Taiwan do not want a polarization of relations such as existed in the 1950s. Commerce across the Taiwan Straits has boomed in the 1990s, despite the fact that neither side recognizes the other officially and that trade has to take place through third parties.

The response of the People's Republic has been both carrots and sticks. It has agreed to talks with 'unofficial' representatives of Taiwan. It welcomes trade and investment. But it has never renounced its claim to use force to 'recover' Taiwan under certain circumstances. Recently it has explicitly renewed its threat to intervene militarily if Taiwan does indeed declare independence.

So, as well as taking off in economic terms, will Taiwan 'take off' politically from the rest of China? That is the other question underlying the title of this book, which focuses upon three main themes: first, it considers the political evolution of Taiwan; secondly, it assesses the economic success of the island and asks what the prospects are for continued rapid economic growth; and, finally, it examines Taiwan's external relations, as well as its relations with the mainland.

Chapter 2

Domestic political change

Hermann Halbeisen and Peter Ferdinand

Domestic politics, 1949–87: from hard to soft authoritarianism

When the Nationalists took over Taiwan in 1945, they found an island just recovering from fifty years of Japanese colonial rule. The inhabitants were divided along several lines apart from the divide between the traditional elites and the rest: those who had collaborated with the Japanese and those who had resisted them, those who spoke Fukienese and those who spoke Hakka, and divisions according to the place on the mainland from which their ancestors had originally come. The Nationalists then added a further division. The way in which they took control not merely of the administration but also of the businesses of former Japanese 'collaborators' set the local 'Taiwanese' (i.e. all those who had been living on the island before 1945, irrespective of where their ancestors had come from) against the 'mainlanders'.

The local military commander, General Chen Yi, tried to keep order and, fearing communist infiltration, he ruled with an iron hand. Feelings between Taiwanese and mainlanders became inflamed, and on 28 February 1947 they erupted. As police tried to arrest a woman illegally selling cigarettes in a market, people nearby tried to stop them. The incident escalated and shots were fired, followed by demonstrations which went on for several days. By the end up to 20,000 people had been killed or had disappeared.

The trauma of this event still underlies politics on Taiwan. Although the governor was replaced, the government hushed up the affair. It was only in the early 1990s that President Lee Teng-hui felt able to reopen the question of what exactly had occurred and to offer apologies and some compensation to the families of the victims.

In 1949, when the Nationalist government was forced finally to abandon the mainland, about one and a half million people fled to Taiwan. The local population numbered around seven million, and so mainlanders accounted for nearly one-fifth of the total. They kept a tight control on power, declaring that the Republic of China had been forced to move to Taiwan but was still the same government of the whole of China.

The Nationalists re-created on Taiwan the network of national political institutions which had previously ruled China from Nanking. They re-established the five-*yuan* (chamber) structure of government which Sun Yat-sen had set up in the first Nationalist government in the 1920s. The role of the Legislative Yuan (LY) or elected legislature was supplemented by the National Assembly (NA), which met rarely, acting as an electoral college for the President and the Vice-President, as well as possessing powers to amend the constitution. The Executive Yuan (EY), the equivalent of a cabinet of ministers, was responsible for the execution of policy. The Judicial Yuan (JY) was the equivalent of a supreme court. The Examination Yuan (ExY) organized civil-service examinations and awarded professional licences. Finally the Control Yuan (CY), indirectly elected by provincial and municipal councils, was intended to monitor the performance of government officials and prevent corruption.

On the basis of the claim that they were still the government of the whole of China, the Nationalists declared that the elected legislature should continue to consist of the representatives chosen throughout China on a province-by-province basis in the elections of 1947. Taiwan was but one of thirty provinces and, though regular elections were held, its representatives were always in a small minority in the LY. In the other provinces, by-elections were held only to replace representatives who died or became incapacitated. This situation persisted until 1992.

The structure was designed to keep the Kuomintang (KMT) or Nationalist Party in power and forestall any challenges. The KMT's grip was all the tighter because of a symbiotic relationship with the army high command – the party had a system of political commissars inside the armed forces as well as in the civilian administration to ensure political control – based on a common fear of infiltration from the mainland. Martial law remained in force until 1987 and was used to suppress not only communist sympathizers, but anyone who expressed even mildly critical views of the regime in public. It was also used to prevent workers striking. The economy was managed on a semi-corporatist basis, through a number of 'peak' organizations representing capital and labour, but controlled by the KMT.

At the highest levels it seemed as though nothing had changed. Chiang Kai-shek was still Chairman of the KMT and approved all top personnel changes. As a result central executive posts were dominated by party members. On the other hand, at lower levels the party had in a sense to be reborn. Its grassroots civilian organization had been lost in the move to Taiwan, since only soldiers and officials associated with the regime had come. There could be no such organization on Taiwan itself because the Nationalists had only operated there since 1945. Only the party cells inside the army had been preserved. It is estimated that in 1950 the party had around 50,000 members, but by 1952 that figure had risen to around 282,000.[1]

The KMT found ways of inserting itself into Taiwanese society, to enhance its legitimacy and to reduce the need for repression to dispose of opposition. It did this by seeking to appeal to leaders of local opinion and encouraging them to join the party. Sometimes this involved co-opting local factions, which had coalesced on the basis of local language, territory or loyalty to individual leaders. Since the party directed mobilization for elections, both local and provincial, it could offer opportunities to those who joined to become elected and thereby demonstrate that it offered rewards in the form of higher status. And sometimes the party performed a task of social integration by mediating between factions and ensuring, as far as possible, that all derived some benefits from cooperation. Furthermore, by tapping already existing networks, it legitimized and raised their status. Thus the party and local factions became dependent on each other in a process of KMT adaptation to Taiwanese society which began early, if slowly.

The party began to 'Taiwanize' itself towards the end of the 1950s. The majority of members were still those who had come from the mainland and it remained the case that mainlanders dominated the top levels of the party, but gradually increasing numbers of Taiwanese began to join at the bottom as well. And since the pool of mainlanders from whom party members could be drawn was necessarily finite as no one could leave the mainland after 1949, the Taiwanese gradually came to outnumber them. At the beginning of the 1970s party membership reached one million, and at roughly that time Taiwanese began to outnumber mainlanders. A decade later the total figure was two million, and at the end of the 1980s nearly three million, which represented roughly 13 per cent of the total population.

As long as Chiang Kai-shek was alive, change in the party took place slowly and beneath the surface. The political system remained opaque, and the constitution was no guide to the way in which actual decisions were taken.[2] His most important position was not President of the Republic of China but Chairman of the KMT. After his death in 1975, and especially after the emergence of his son, Chiang Ching-kuo, as President in 1978, change began to take place both more rapidly and more openly.

International developments also played a role. The decision by the USA in 1972 to recognize the People's Republic of China and to distance itself from the ROC weakened the domestic credibility of the Nationalist regime. Then the US decision to abandon its defence agreement with the ROC in 1979 and upgrade its representation in Peking to full ambassadorial level at the expense of any official recognition of Taiwan concentrated the minds of Taiwanese leaders on how to re-establish themselves on the international stage. Democratic reform was one way of achieving this.

Chiang Ching-kuo personally set about introducing new and younger blood into the higher reaches of the regime, in part at least to consolidate his position with his own loyal followers. This also involved the promotion of greater numbers of 'Taiwanese', a policy he became convinced was needed if the stability of the regime was to be preserved. Symbolically this was expressed in his decision in the 1980s to choose as his Vice-President Lee Teng-hui, a Taiwanese agricultural economist trained in the USA and former Governor of Taiwan province. A broader picture, however, can be gained from Table 2.1.

Table 2.1 Key characteristics of KMT cadres, 1975 and 1985 (%)

	Province		County		District	
	1975	1985	1975	1985	1975	1985
Average age	n.a.	47.0	43.7	43.8	38.1	35.5
Place of birth						
Taiwan	n.a.	27.9	34.5	53.9	56.6	73.3
Mainland	n.a.	72.1	65.4	46.1	43.4	26.7
Gender						
Male	n.a.	76.6	82.6	84.1	92.0	94.6
Female	n.a.	23.4	17.4	15.9	8.0	5.4

Source: Yang Dezhang, 'Tangkung jenli chiekou chi toshao?', *Shuangshi Yuan*, no. 15 (15 March 1985), pp. 37–41, cited in Dickson, 'The Adaptability of Leninist Parties', p. 276.

As Chiang Ching-kuo assumed greater power, pressures for more rapid democratization built up. In local elections in 1977, the KMT did not do particularly well. It lost ground to a number of candidates who were standing as independents but had loosely coordinated policy positions and who were called by the press the Tangwai group (i.e. people outside the party). Their success encouraged them to try to organize themselves. In 1979 a demonstration between police and oppositionists in Kaohsiung turned violent and led to the arrest and imprisonment of leaders of opposition factions. But far from polarizing the situation, the effect was that both the KMT and the opposition pulled back from confrontation.

During the 1980s further developments on the mainland and in East Asia helped to make democratization politically acceptable. The peaceful victory of Mrs Aquino over President Marcos in the Philippines had been a powerful demonstration of 'people power' in the region. And on the mainland the change from Maoist extremism towards Deng Xiaoping's pragmatic economic reforms reduced the apparent threat of invasion. This was vital for democratization in Taiwan, allowing a relaxation of controls on the opposition to get onto the political agenda.

A prerequisite for change was the development of Taiwanese society as a result of rapid economic growth over the preceding twenty-five years. A more prosperous middle class had emerged which wanted greater personal freedom. Young people were disdainful of old-fashioned ideology, elderly leaders and tight controls. Many went abroad to study and stayed there. Taiwanese businessmen were more self-confident as a result of their business success. And the distinction between Taiwanese and mainlanders became less salient with the emergence of an entire new generation that was born on the island and intermarried. People were becoming more receptive to the idea of change, although they were not yet ready to press for it.

Crucial in all this was the personal contribution of Chiang Ching-kuo. It was his growing conviction that democratic reforms were needed to ensure the continuity of the regime after his death, and also, possibly, to ensure a favourable assessment of his rule by future historians. There were still enough conservative-minded figures in the top ranks of the KMT to obstruct reform if Chiang Ching-kuo had not pushed it through. In June 1986 he convened a study group to consider various crucial political initiatives. This encouraged the Tangwai group to form their own political party, the Democratic Progressive Party, even though it was still illegal to do so.

In 1987 Chiang Ching-kuo began to implement reform by rescinding the martial law regulations, thus opening the way for more open politics.

The redistribution of political influence

Chiang Ching-kuo's sudden death in January 1988 unleashed a series of far-reaching changes in Taiwan's domestic politics. It also marked the end of a political dynasty. Disproving countless rumours and apprehensions that his two youngest sons, Chiang Hsiao-wu and Chiang Hsiao-yang, might be groomed as successors by conservative groups within the military and the party apparatus, neither of them was able to build his own power base and to reach a position within the hierarchy that would allow him to play an important role after his father's death. The promotion of President Chiang Ching-kuo's younger brother, Chiang Wei-kuo, to the position of Secretary General of the National Security Council ensured the smooth succession to office of the legal successor, but it did not provide Chiang Wei-kuo with a stepping-stone to a new career in politics. With two of Chiang Ching-kuo's three sons now dead, and the remaining son concentrating on the management of party-related business companies, and with Madame Chiang Kai-shek living permanently in the USA, the influence that the Chiang family could exert on Taiwan's political development became minimal. Only the two illegitimate sons of Chiang Ching-kuo, Chang Hsiao-yen and Chang Hsiao-ssu, both members of the KMT's Central Committee (CC), continue to play minor roles.

With the death of Chiang Ching-kuo both the KMT and the state apparatus lost their power centre. Unlike his father Chiang Kai-shek, who provided his eldest son with a long training period to gain both the experience and the political base needed for an eventual succession to the apex of power, Chiang Ching-kuo did not groom a designated successor possessing similar qualifications. Under these circumstances a realignment of power within the Nationalist system became unavoidable.

Chiang Ching-kuo's successor as President of the Republic and – after some initial opposition – as Chairman of the KMT, Lee Teng-hui, was distinguished by an outstanding career as a technocrat and a complete lack of affiliation to any of the numerous factions of mainlander or Taiwanese politicians. Though he had only joined the KMT in 1972, these qualifications made him acceptable to, if not a first choice for, all currents within the KMT, but left him without any power base besides the authority of his office and his popularity with the public.

9

The realignment of power among the leading personalities of the regime and the main currents of the party was complicated by a number of contending influences. Several powerful groups were competing against one another, e.g. Taiwanese against mainlanders, elected members of representative institutions against technocrats and party cadres, politicians whose influence depended to a considerable degree upon the backing of Chiang Ching-kuo against those possessing a base among the party membership or in other organizations.

The KMT on Taiwan had observed meticulously the procedural rules for filling high offices. Thus Lee Teng-hui's succession as President was unopposed. His nomination as temporary Chairman of the KMT, however, encountered the opposition of conservative mainlanders. Although this challenge was quickly overcome, it marked the beginning of a series of conflicts concerning the choice of personnel and policies, which resulted in a broad realignment of various groups within the KMT into the so-called 'main current' (*chu liu*) and 'secondary current' (*fei chu liu*).

Membership has fluctuated over the years, but it is the main current that supports President Lee and his political programme. It consists mainly of Taiwanese politicians, mostly present or former members of the representative bodies, and a number of mainlanders interested in securing their present position through cooperation with up-and-coming local groups. The secondary current enjoyed (until their retirement in December 1991) the support of a considerable number of the older representatives in the LY, elected on the mainland in 1947 and 1948. It comprises mostly leading members of the party and administrative apparatuses, mainlanders as well as Taiwanese, whose political influence is endangered by the process of democratization, and a number of younger politicians of mainland origin, technocrats within the administration as well as elected representatives, whose chances of political advancement are jeopardized by the ongoing Taiwanization process.

In addition to the struggle for power and influence, symbolic politics also had an impact on relations between the two currents – namely, attitudes towards one of the main tenets of Nationalist rule, commitment to the one-China policy. For the first time since 1949 the two most important offices in the ROC were occupied by a person not born on the Chinese mainland; someone, moreover, whose political outlook was shaped neither by the experiences of the Nationalist struggle against Japan nor by the civil war with the Chinese Communists. A number of conservatives harboured doubts about President Lee's commitment to the Nationalist state's aims for reunification and Taiwan's identity as part of China. Whereas the secondary current emphatically upheld reunification as the final aim of the KMT, the main current displayed a more detached attitude. In their campaigns for election to the LY, a number of candidates from the main current publicly supported the idea of 'one Taiwan, one China'.

The struggle between these two currents reached a climax during preparations for the presidential elections in the spring of 1990. Confronted by a majority of conservative senior representatives in the National Assembly, which acts as an electoral college to choose the President, President Lee was forced to dispel any doubts concerning his continuing commitment to the Nationalist agenda in order to obtain their support. In spite of intensive campaigning on his part and a pledge to convoke a commission that would deliberate on ways to reunite the nation, the so-called National Unification Commission (*Kuochi t'ungi weiyuanhui*), his position was challenged after his election by a second candidate, put up by a number of senior right-wing representatives with strong loyalties to the Chiang family. This challenge brought together one of the main political rivals of Lee Teng-hui, Lin Ying-kang, also a native Taiwanese and Chairman of the Judicial Yuan, with Chiang Wei-kuo as the vice-presidential candidate, to match the presidential ticket of Lee Teng-hui and Lee Yuan-tzu, a mainlander and former Justice Minister. It was only after the intervention of a group of senior party leaders and public support for Lee Teng-hui's candidacy from Chiang Ching-kuo's son, Hsiao-wu, that the intraparty opposition withdrew its challenge.

The attempts of the secondary current to prevent the abandonment of the traditional agenda of nationalistic policy and to maintain the existing political structure dominated the deliberations of the Third Plenum of the Twelfth CC of the KMT in spring 1992. Convened to consider amendments to the constitution and a change in the method of electing the president, the Plenum turned into a confrontation between the two currents. The proposal for direct presidential elections, supported by President Lee and the delegates belonging to the main current, was criticized vehemently by members of the secondary current, who feared for the future role of the NA within the political system of the ROC once such a change was accepted, but who were opposed even more to tinkering with a fundamental feature of the constitution.

The continuing struggle between the two currents has also manifested itself in disputes between the incumbents of the two most important

11

executive offices of the ROC: the president and the premier. President Lee, the foremost representative of the main current, failed to obtain the premier's office for a member of his group. He succeeded in replacing Yu Kuo-hua, the long-serving Premier under the presidency of Chiang Ching-kuo and considered an arch-conservative; but his choice for the office, Lee Huan, like Yu a trusted aide of Chiang Ching-kuo and acting Secretary-General of the KMT, could also be considered a traditionalist within the party. Against a background of considerable public hopes for more harmonious leadership, the relationship between the two leaders soon ran into irreconcilable political differences. After only 16 months Lee Huan was replaced as premier.

The President's choice as replacement, Hao Pei-ts'un, also a mainlander and a former army chief of staff, was considered even more conservative than his predecessors. His nomination caused considerable disillusionment among the President's supporters and led to a wave of public protests, inspired both by opposition to the continuing influence of conservative mainlanders and by apprehension about the growing role of the armed forces in political life. Under the premiership of Hao Pei-ts'un, the tensions between the two currents became more visible, both because of Hao's outspokenness and in the intensified competition between the presidential office and the EY over the power to decide the political agenda. Subsequently Hao complained about Lee's authoritarian style of decision-making. After the elections of 1992, Lee felt able to replace him with a premier who was closer to his views, Lien Chan.

Political reforms and disruptions in policy-making

The impact of political reforms and the declining authority of the presidential office after the death of Chiang Ching-kuo affected relations between national political institutions and the policy-making process in a number of ways. Problems arising from the personalities of the President and the Premier and from the transitional process were exacerbated by structural inconsistencies in constitutional relations between institutions.

Since 1987 the President has lost a number of powers to the Premier. Thus the presidency no longer represents the power centre of the political system but has been reduced to being *primus inter pares*, one important institution among several others. This does not imply that the conduct of affairs will become easier; quite the contrary. It may be argued that in future the president will have to combine the demands of being a leading representative of a political party with the task of symbolic representation of national unity. The current incumbent, President Lee, seems to have opted for a more detached role, distancing himself somewhat from partisan politics.

Yet public opinion and the majority of the population do not fully appreciate these changes. They continue to perceive the presidency as the most influential institution in the policy-making process, a position they came to accept as self-evident during the rule of Chiang Kai-shek and Chiang Ching-kuo. The increasing number of conflicts between President Lee and Premier Hao, resulting from the latter's more combative style, which diverged sharply from the low-profile bureaucratic approach of his predecessors, as well as from considerable differences in outlook, were seen as exceptions to the norm.

The relationship between the Executive Yuan and the Legislative Yuan is also undergoing rapid changes, with the LY playing an increasing role in the policy-making process, thereby reasserting rights that it surrendered during the 1970s as most of its members aged. In the opinion of some of its critics at that time, the LY was transformed into a legislative office of the EY, which simply received draft bills formulated by the EY and passed them into law without much deliberation. This was despite a limited influx of new and more active representatives.

Although the LY has succeeded in reasserting some of its influence *vis-à-vis* the executive in the past decade, this development has been circumscribed by a number of structural factors. One is the very limited availability of resources within the LY, which deprives the individual representative of the professional advice needed to put him on an equal footing with the expertise of the administration. The system of parliamentary committees, moreover, displays serious deficiencies. Since there is no scheme assuring an adequate membership level in all committees, representatives tend to concentrate on the few committees they deem to be most relevant to their particular interests, leaving the less popular ones unable to function properly.

The policy-making process still leaves a great deal of scope for the KMT apparatus to coordinate and supervise implementation of decisions made by the state. Decisions defining the executive's political priorities, and sometimes even the details of policies deemed to be of special importance by the Nationalist leadership, are taken during meetings of the KMT's Central Standing Committee (CSC). After a decision is made in the CSC, the Central Political Commission and the leadership of the party branch in the LY are entrusted with obtaining the support of the representatives. Consultation between the EY and members of the LY prior to the introduction of a draft bill is usual in cases where special interests are concerned. Compromises reconciling conflicts between the EY and the LY also fall within the scope of the Central Political Commission.

There also remain some problems in the work of the LY. For one thing, the term of office of representatives has been fixed at only three years. Since a significant part of the last year is overshadowed by the forthcoming re-election campaign, this means that in practice only two years are available for proper legislative deliberation.

A second problem is the simmering dispute between the National Assembly and the Legislative Yuan about their appropriate roles in the Republic's power structure. Flaring up periodically, this adversarial relationship was enflamed by the second constitutional amendment in 1992. Not content with their role as members of an electoral college and under continuing pressure to demonstrate their usefulness, the members of the NA have repeatedly tried to enlarge its jurisdiction at the expense of the LY. Some of these attempts have been abandoned under strong pressure from the KMT, but a constitutional amendment adopted in September 1994 gave the NA the right to elect its own speaker and deputy speaker and to exercise its powers according to its own decisions. In addition, the character of the NA is itself changing. KMT intraparty loyalty and the authority of the leadership are both declining and it will be difficult for the party to maintain the same degree of control, especially if, as some predict, it loses its two-thirds majority in the 1996 elections.

On the other hand the LY has regularly attempted to use its budgetary powers to assert its authority over the NA. One fundamental issue is the difference in attitude of the two main parties over the most appropriate form for constitutional arrangements. The KMT wishes to preserve the old five-chamber system. The DPP wishes to move towards a Western-type democracy. As the electoral gap between these parties narrows, the possibility of compromise diminishes. Thus the likelihood of disputes over constitutional issues is increasing, despite the fact that three rounds of constitutional amendments have been approved since the move towards democracy at the end of the 1980s.

The impact of the emerging civil society

The end of martial law gave space to, and opened new avenues of influence for, a number of forces in Taiwanese society. Developing during the decades of socio-economic change, various social forces first attempted to reduce the control the political centre exerted on them and later began to formulate their own political demands. Over the long term economic growth had provided a number of groups with the resources needed for a successful articulation of their demands. The end of martial law allowed these groups to voice them.

Newspapers and magazines provided a sounding board that amplified hitherto unreported demands. With the end of martial law a number of restrictions regulating the size and the establishment of newspapers and magazines became ineffective. In response to the new freedoms numerous newspapers and magazines were founded and they considerably enlarged the spectrum of opinions that could be published. Even newspapers close to the KMT were forced to change their editorial policies and report on topics that only a few years previously they would have left for opposition papers with limited circulations to take up.

During the 1990s officialdom has increasingly been challenged by private radio stations, usually operating illegally, without a licence. Sometimes they have dared the police to come and arrest them, only to set up their transmitters elsewhere immediately afterwards. Broadcasting usually in Fukienese or Hakka rather than Mandarin, they have played a significant part in crystallizing the self-identity of non-mainlanders.

Although changes in the media made the dissemination of dissenting views and opinions easier, the medium with the greatest impact on the public, television, was largely excluded from liberalization. TV stations on Taiwan are still under the tight control of the KMT and the government. Several efforts to present the public with different interpretations of political events were undertaken by independent teams of reporters in 1989 and 1992. Although they distributed videotapes of election campaigns widely throughout the island once opposition parties were legalized, their efforts failed to have a lasting effect on public opinion. The establishment of an illegal TV station by the DPP during the 1989 LY elections met with a similar fate. In more recent years, however, the growth of cable television has meant that independent TV companies can now broadcast their own news programmes, effectively breaking the government's control over political reporting.

Numerous demonstrations attest to the increasing efforts of groups within Taiwanese society to present demands to the political elites, which they regard as ill-informed and indifferent to public opinion. Protests organized by university students against the delays caused by elderly parliamentarians in the reform process and their support for an opposition ticket during the 1990 presidential elections attracted widespread attention, while the campaign against the nomination of Hao Pei-ts'un as premier revealed widespread apprehension among the politically active population about the militarization of political life.

Enlarged freedom of public opinion permitted the public debate of topics that had formerly been discussed only in small circles, in a number of radical magazines with a limited circulation. These included the idea of a Taiwanese identity different from that of mainland China, as well as demands for a Taiwanese state. The debate began to widen when political liberalization permitted the return of adherents of the Taiwan Independence Movement. A change in the editorial policy of a well-known publishing house, the Independence Newspaper Group (*Tzuli paohsi*), which moved on from supporting democratization and liberalization to propagating a decidedly Taiwanese point of view, spread these ideas to an even larger public.

Discussion of a Taiwanese identity, originally limited to questions of politics, spread to culture, language and history. A group of authors dedicated to the use of Taiwanese languages established a second PEN Club on the island, membership of which excluded authors using Mandarin. Considerable efforts were undertaken to prove the existence of a Taiwanese historical consciousness different from that of the continental Chinese and to reconstruct the history of Taiwan from a Taiwanese point of view. Efforts by several conservative associations to counter what they perceived as a growing identification on the part of the KMT with Taiwan and its readiness to relinquish the aim of reunification made little impact and subsided after a few months.

These activities could be interpreted as a reaction to the abolition of long-established restrictions. A new level of criticism was reached, however, when groups of intellectuals and civic-minded members of the public began to organize associations with the explicit aim of monitoring the performance of political parties and institutions, establishing standards that were not informed by limited political interests and advancing alternatives to policies proposed by the government. For example, taking the Fabian Society as its model, a group of university professors established the Teng-she Society with the aim of raising the standards of political debate. Its articles and commentaries now appear regularly in a number of publications. In the autumn of 1992 the Foundation for Observation of the National Parliaments (*Kuo hui kuanch'a chichinhui*) was established as a reaction to growing factional strife and cosy relations between elected representatives and special-interest groups. A number of private 'think-tanks' have also been established to analyse government policies and formulate alternatives to various government proposals.

At the beginning of the 1980s a number of movements began to take shape, addressing a vast array of social problems. They included the highly specific demands of a small religious association claiming access to a holy mountain situated inside a restricted military area. In general, however, they took up causes that affected large groups of people such as the millions of consumers living on Taiwan. Although some of these groups are able to muster considerable resources and have challenged government policies on several occasions, their long-term impact has not been particularly effective. A few of the spontaneous or locally based self-help movements have gained considerable public attention, e.g. the campaign against the establishment of a chemical factory by a well-known multinational company near the ancient port city of Lukang and the blockade of a Taiwanese chemical complex in Kaohsiung by villagers suffering from pollution. They did not, however, lead to a general increase in support for environmental protection organizations. The number of conflicts and protests related to environmental issues is very likely to increase further in the future, given Taiwan's considerable problems arising from such matters as waste disposal, reliance on nuclear power plants to generate electricity, and the detrimental effects of the government's industrial policies. Nevertheless a fundamental change in attitudes towards the environment either within the government or among the public at large does not seem imminent.

The government has displayed a shrewd flexibility to forestall the demands made by social movements, complying with some of them and creating new governmental bodies such as commissions for labour relations and environmental problems.

Among the social movements gaining in strength during the past decade, the labour movement had been expected to profit most from the end of martial law restrictions. Within the structure of the authoritarian Nationalist regime, labour unions were formally incorporated into the state's decision-making process, although the scope of their activities and their prospects for development were severely circumscribed. Government policy permitted only one organization within a specific sector to represent its interests, and all attempts to create competing representative organizations were immediately suppressed. Growing discontent with trade unions and with the perceived passivity of the trade union council in particular was headed off by both the KMT and the government. The KMT established new institutions dealing specifically with labour issues in the EY and formulated a number of proposals addressing labour problems, including co-optation of individual labour leaders to serve on government or party bodies.

Efforts to raise the political consciousness of Taiwanese workers or to provide more effective representation of their interests by forming new associations have met with only limited success. Some initial achievements quickly lost momentum due to a strategy of accommodation on the part of the KMT and the realities of economic organization on Taiwan. Neither the activities of several leftist groups, the most effective of them being affiliated with a radical publication from the Tangwai era (*Hsia ch'ao*) or with the 'New Movement' faction (*Hsin ch'aoliu*) of the DPP, nor the establishment of two political parties intended to promote the cause of the working classes brought results, because the working class lacked a sufficiently developed consciousness of shared interests.

Elections and political change

Elections at local or regional level have taken place regularly since the 1950s. The number of vacancies filled by newcomers in elections increased steadily over the years, a result of Taiwan's growing population, but remained lower than the number of seats occupied by elderly representatives. Despite lacking a decisive influence on the distribution of power, elections have become an important instrument facilitating the integration of new social and economic groups into the political system.

During the past three decades these opportunities have been taken mostly by Taiwanese, although increasing participation by mainlanders has been noted since the middle of the 1980s.

Elections were accorded increasing importance as a way to strengthen – and to demonstrate to the outside world – the legitimacy of the KMT's continuing rule over the island. Thus the party invested considerable resources, both personal and material, in election campaigns in order to achieve favourable results. Over the years these efforts made the KMT one of the few authoritarian parties in the world to organize – and win – electoral campaigns against fairly strong competition.

As in Japan, elections to most seats are on the basis of multi-member territorial constituencies. There are 26 of these, based upon the cities and counties of Taiwan province, with the special municipalities of Taipei and Kaohsiung each divided into two constituencies. In each constituency between one and 16 seats are contested, depending on the size of the population. A measure of proportional representation has been added with the introduction of a national constituency and one for overseas Chinese living abroad. In both cases candidates are elected from a national party list. The seats are then allocated on a proportional basis to all parties that have gained a minimum of 5 per cent of the total votes.

Since the number of territorial constituencies is smaller than the number of seats, the political parties are forced to nominate more than one candidate in the larger constituencies if they want to achieve a majority of seats. A successful electoral strategy in the past was based on a fairly precise estimation of the party's share of the votes in a given constituency and its ability to allocate a fairly equal number of votes to each of its candidates. Under those circumstances the KMT enjoyed a number of advantages given its superior organizational abilities and the existence in the electorate of groups whose voting behaviour closely followed the advice of the party branch. Thus the KMT's share of seats normally exceeded its share of the vote by a considerable margin.

Changes in society have considerably reduced the number of groups of voters open to manipulation; at the same time more candidates have appeared with the means to wage their own electoral campaigns. Thus the opportunities for the party apparatus to allocate votes and to control the number of candidates have been reduced. While this enhances the electoral chances of the individual party candidates, it also increases the need for each candidate to distinguish himself or herself from competing candidates of the same party. But the increasing dispersal of votes among growing numbers of candidates also gives a better chance of success to independent candidates with strong local roots or representing special interests.

As a result candidates are relying more on their own resources rather than party headquarters for running and financing their campaigns. They have their own support groups and they raise money for themselves. Indeed some KMT candidates disclaim any connection with the party's headquarters because they fear being tainted with the general suspicion of corruption. Whatever the party rules may say about the obligation to democratic centralism among party members, there is little that the party leadership can do to enforce it. In 1992 the KMT tried to bar the nomination of some prominent dissidents but only succeeded in making them more popular.

During the second half of the 1980s a number of trends became discernible in both the pre-electoral and the election campaigns. The number of candidates participating in the elections increased steadily, as did the number of party members – or members of the Tangwai – competing for nomination as official candidates. This upsurge in participation made changes in the nomination procedures necessary. The DPP organized primaries and had party members choose from a slate of candidates, while the KMT opted for a mixture of intraparty primaries and final selection of candidates by a small group of party leaders. These measures failed effectively to limit the number of candidates in both parties, since those who were unsuccessful in their bid for nomination often participated in the elections regardless of their party's decision.

As a consequence of fiercer competition the expenditure on electoral campaigns has increased immensely. In December 1992 observers reported that a candidate would have to spend at least NT$100 million, equivalent to nearly US$4 million, in order to run a promising campaign.[3] More and more politicians will have to seek financial support either from local factions (*tifang p'aihsi*) combining political and economic interests, or from large business groups. The number of candidates belonging to successful entrepreneurial families is also on the increase.

The diverging interests of the political parties, local factions and other groups create new tensions. They are intensified by the demands of a successful campaign in a single-vote/multi-member constituency. In order to distinguish themselves from other competitors of the same party, candidates of both the DPP and the KMT have formed subgroups, running under different names with their own small political platforms and campaign organizations. Similarities with the activities of local support groups for individual candidates of parties in Japan (*koenkai*) have become quite obvious.

During the election campaign in 1989 the DPP and the KMT used quite different programmes to attract votes. Whereas the KMT favoured less explicit themes related to the ideas of prosperity, welfare and security, the DPP made explicit demands for further democratization and speedy political reforms. Halfway through the campaign a new topic arose after a number of DPP candidates argued in favour of Taiwanese independence: the issue of Taiwan's international status.

The results of the elections confirmed some trends observed in the LY elections of 1986. These and subsequent election results can be seen in Table 2.2.

In 1989 the DPP succeeded in consolidating its position as the main force in the opposition, its share of the votes increasing from 22.8 per cent to 28.6 per cent. The KMT suffered painful losses. Its share of the votes, which had been in decline since the beginning of the decade, fell

Table 2.2 Share of votes by political parties in nationwide elections, 1989–94 (%)

	KMT	DPP	New Party
Legislative Yuan, 1989	60.9	28.6	
City mayors and magistrates, 1989	52.7	38.3	
National Assembly, 1991	69.1	23.2	
Legislative Yuan, 1992	61.7	36.1	
City mayors and magistrates, 1993	47.3	41.2	3.1
Taiwan provincial governorship, 1994	56.2	38.7	4.3
Legislative Yuan, 1995	46.1	33.2	13.0

Source: Shenn-Pyng Luo, 'The Politics of Restructuring: The Taiwan Case' (PhD thesis, University of Essex, 1994), p. 172; *Far Eastern Economic Review* 14 December 1995, p. 15. For a fuller analysis of the 1995 results, see for example the *Central Daily News*, 4 December 1995.

by 9 per cent, from 69.9 per cent to 60.9 per cent. The number of votes cast for independent candidates continued to increase, from 7.2 per cent to 8.9 per cent. The DPP was less successful when it came to transforming votes into seats. Although the party· obtained 21 mandates, this represented only 20.8 per cent of seats contested, while the KMT received 72 mandates, equivalent to 71.3 per cent. The KMT needed only 66,166 votes to win a seat, whereas the DPP needed 106,726.

The results of the NA elections of 1991 display a number of changes. Although these elections were the first to take place under the new set of regulations contained in the first constitutional amendment and were of considerable importance for the future course of political reform, both the DPP and the KMT encountered difficulties in motivating qualified persons to take part. Since the NA exerts little influence on the decision-making process, few well-known politicians were willing to participate. Therefore both parties nominated a considerable number of local dignitaries and personalities only loosely affiliated with them. In a number of cases both the qualifications and the loyalties of the elected representatives were open to doubt.

The DPP tried to focus its electoral campaign on one topic – the procedures for the election of the President and Vice-President – and it organized its campaign around its demand for direct elections. This strategy failed to attract the attention of the electorate, however, and the DPP suffered heavy losses, while the KMT increased its percentage of the vote. In addition to the KMT and the DPP, and apart from independent candidates, only one other party, the Chinese Social Democratic Party (CSDP), was able to field candidates in nearly all constituencies. The elections also saw another new development. Reacting to the new rules regulating the distribution of indirect mandates, a ticket of independent candidates was organized.

A total of 667 candidates competed for 325 seats, of which 225 were filled by direct elections, 80 were in the national constituency and 20 were reserved for overseas Chinese. Only 16 out of 62 political parties had nominated one or more candidates. The KMT increased its share of the vote to 69.1 per cent and won a total of 254 seats, while the DPP's share dropped to 23.2 per cent, which assured it of 66 seats in the NA. Five independent candidates also won a seat. Neither the ticket of independent candidates, with a share of 2.16 per cent, nor the CSDP, which participated in the elections for the first time, with a share of 2.08 per cent, was able to win any indirect mandates.[4]

The growth of subgroups and factions among the candidates of the large parties continued unabated. Intense efforts by the KMT party leadership to stop this process by denying several prominent representatives of such groups a renewed nomination failed. The candidates, in addition to their affiliations with the large factions in the party, created further subgroups for campaign purposes.

The election platforms of both the KMT and the DPP displayed many similarities with those of earlier campaigns. The KMT stressed its successful policies in economic development and its commitment to guarantee domestic stability, and promised more of the same for the future, adopting the triad 'stability, prosperity and confidence' as its campaign slogan. The DPP for its part maintained a critical attitude towards the government and demanded further political reforms. Its campaign slogan contained three demands for sovereignty, direct election of the president and tax reductions – and three objections, opposing the growing influence of money on politics, the influence of the military on domestic politics, and the special rights enjoyed by certain groups.

In the campaign for the 1992 LY elections, the DPP had learnt its lesson from the failures of 1991 and muted its stance on the international status of Taiwan. Instead of independence, it now called for 'one China, one Taiwan'. It also declared that if it won a majority it would propose a national referendum on the issue, and only if it gained positive endorsement would it proceed further. It concentrated on issues of corruption in the KMT, the dangers of military rule and of privileges. The DPP's case was strengthened by a number of scandals which came to light. In addition it sought popularity by advocating more social programmes. Having in previous elections clearly established an identity as a party in favour of Taiwanese independence, the DPP then broadened that appeal to attract more voters. The KMT, on the other hand, targeted its campaign strategy on business groups. This significantly alienated voters, and the KMT's share of the vote fell.

In December 1994 there were local elections for the posts of governor of Taiwan and the mayors of Taipei and Kaohsiung. Here the KMT did well to hold on to the governorship and the mayoralty of Kaohsiung, while the DPP candidate became mayor of Taipei. In the capital the KMT was penalized by the electorate for incompetence in building up the city's infrastructure, as well as for suspected connivance at fraud in public works contracts. The DPP had shown that it could win an important election in which the international status of Taiwan was not really at issue, and that it had succeeded in turning itself into a genuine opposition party.

Then in the December 1995 elections the KMT's share of the vote sank to its lowest level ever. It still won a majority of seats in the LY, i.e. 85 out of 164, but this was a fall of eleven compared with the 1992 elections (though then there had been only 161 seats). As can be seen from Table 1.2, the total vote for the KMT was almost exactly equal to that of the two chief opposition parties combined. On the other hand the DPP, too, did less well than it had hoped. Although its seats increased by four, its share of the vote went up by only 2 per cent. The chief winners were the New Party, created in 1993, which opposed both the pro-independence line of the DPP and the corruption of the KMT. The party originally comprised seven former KMT LY representatives who had defected in 1993; after the elections, however, it had a total of 21 representatives.

Subsequent analysis suggested that the chief reasons for this were the intensified association of the KMT with corruption (during the campaign a KMT representative in the provincial assembly was convicted of vote-buying during previous elections) and a suspicion that the DPP had focused too much on the independence issue while neglecting more routine domestic policy concerns. By contrast the New Party seemed to have attracted support from younger middle-class liberal voters.

Outlines of a new party system

At the end of the 1980s a majority of reform advocates would have opted for a two-party system resembling those of the UK or the USA. The outlines of the new party system that is slowly taking shape on the island, after the lifting of martial law and the legalization of new political parties, do not yet match these expectations.

Within a few months of the amendment of the Law on Civil Organizations in 1988, more than 60 political parties had been established. Only a few of them, however, gained any political importance. After latent intraparty conflicts broke out openly and several alienated groups left the parties to establish new organizations, the 'friendly' parties rapidly disintegrated and lost what was left of their influence. The vast majority of the parties founded after 1988 did not participate in elections, or could only muster a handful of candidates. Only four were able to attract public support, and whether they will succeed in transforming this goodwill into continuous public support remains doubtful.

Two of these new parties were founded by politicians who left the DPP to form their own organizations. Only one year after the DPP had been established, a member of the party's parliamentary party, Wang Yi-hsiung, formed the Labour Party (*Kung tang*), which he envisaged as the political arm of a developing labour movement. The Kung-tang had some initial success in co-opting a number of small labour associations outside and opposed to KMT control. Within a few months, however, differences between the party's two main currents, one organized around the party's founding father, the other consisting mainly of former left-wing activists affiliated with *China Tide* magazine, became irreconcilable. The *China Tide* group left and formed a new organization, the Workers' Party (*Laokung tang*). Although the membership of each party is fairly small (amounting to no more than a few thousand individuals), both consider themselves as representing the interests of the working classes. However, judging by the patterns of nominations for regional and two national elections during recent years, both parties show distinct regional rather than class affiliations. For the 1992 LY elections the Labour Party nominated only one candidate, and the Workers' Party only two.

At the end of the 1980s the CSDP was established by one of Taiwan's most prominent politicians and a former member of the DPP, Chu Kao-chang. Although the party's political platform was modelled on that of the German SPD, the CSDP did not go after the labour vote but saw itself as representative of the better-educated sections of the middle class, a group that has become disenchanted with the KMT over its conservative political orientation and policies favouring large industries, and that is appalled by the radicalism and combativeness of the DPP. Though its membership hovered around 3,000, the CSDP made considerable efforts to field candidates in each of the territorial constituencies for both the 1991 NA and the 1992 LY elections. Nevertheless, when it became clear how difficult it was to grow, the CSDP merged with the third of the larger new dissident parties, the New Party (NP).

Originally a distinct faction within the KMT, called the New KMT Alliance, the New Party split away from the KMT in 1994. It has three distinguishing features. The first is a platform dominated by the issue of Taiwan's international status. The NP definitely wants Taiwan to retain its old one-China policy and has been very critical of President Lee Teng-hui's attempts to change the line on that issue.

The second feature of the NP is its forthright criticism of the 'money politics' which, it says, is the hallmark of the KMT's policies. NP leaders won impressive numbers of votes in elections in 1993 and 1995, on the basis of their demands for a clean-up of Taiwanese politics. In fact, the party's founding statement stressed this issue rather than policy towards the mainland. Its electoral success is particularly striking, given the party's third distinguishing feature – that its representatives are young and of mainlander background. Even though they come from a minority on Taiwan, their anti-corruption appeal seemed to outweigh that disadvantage. As was seen in Table 2.2 the party won only about 5 per cent of the vote for its candidates in the local elections in 1994 and 13 per cent in the LY elections in 1995. Nevertheless its performance was better than that of any other third party. To improve its performance even further in subsequent elections the NP will have to broaden its appeal beyond its political base in the northern part of the island. Its current membership of around 40,000 puts severe constraints on its efforts to find good candidates.

Responses to political change by the KMT and DPP

The KMT

The changing political framework posed different kinds of challenge for the DPP and the KMT. For the KMT the task consisted of reforming a party structured according to the tenets of Marxism-Leninism and providing opportunities both for active participation by party members and for greater influence in policy formation by elected politicians.

In spite of a membership of around 2 million, the overwhelming majority of them now Taiwanese and under the age of 35, the KMT has remained essentially a party run by cadres, with limited intraparty activities for the average member and a dominant role for the leadership in determining the party's political course. The party organization is divided into territorial and sectoral sub-units at the provincial party level. It is maintained by membership fees, and more importantly by the profits of the party's extended business interests. These are shrouded in secrecy, but in June 1995 the party for the first time registered under its own name its shares in seven large holding companies amounting to nearly US$1.5 billion (excluding cash and land holdings which the party also has at its disposal). One estimate suggested that KMT income in 1995 would be worth US$450 million.[5]

Under the chairmanship of Chiang Kai-shek and Chiang Ching-kuo, most decisions on party policy were made by the chairman alone. Even the members of the party's Central Committee and Central Standing Committee were not involved regularly in decision-making. Changes occurred only during the final years of Chiang Ching-kuo's chairmanship when the CSC became more accustomed to debating policy proposals. Under the leadership of Lee Teng-hui this role has been further strengthened, and the CSC has become an important forum for the articulation of conflicting opinions between the party's two main currents.

The KMT's reactions to the continuous changes in the political process on Taiwan have been fairly muted. Neither its political programme nor its organizational structure has undergone any spectacular changes in recent years. During the preparations for the convocation of the party's thirteenth national convention and during the convention itself a hitherto unknown degree of democracy prevailed. A considerable proportion of party delegates were for the first time elected by the membership, as was the CC. But although candid debates took place in the convention's group sessions, new developments in the party's platform did not follow. Irreconcilable differences of opinion concerning the identity and the future tasks of the KMT led to the postponement of structural reforms.

The conservative wing of the party clung to the concept of the KMT as a revolutionary party entrusted with a historical mission and representing the best interests of all strata of society. The reformist groups had a rather different conception of the party's future role. In their opinion the KMT must acknowledge that it is competing for votes with other political parties in greatly changed circumstances if it is to safeguard its position as the ruling party. They tend to envisage the KMT of the future as a conservative, catch-all party. In order to prepare it for this new task, the party organization must be streamlined, by dissolving the numerous suborganizations with overlapping jurisdictions. The restructured party organization would consist of only three branches, dealing with routine business, mobilization, and disciplinary and financial matters. The adoption of such a radical plan would have endangered numerous vested interests, however, and so it was referred back to the members for further deliberations.

Organizational reform and programmatic reformulation thus are two of the tasks that have to be dealt with in the future. Another task still to be accomplished is a realignment of power relations within the party, namely the relative influence of the technocrats and the elected politicians, and also of the mainlanders and Taiwanese. Although the influence of the two last-mentioned groups appears certain to increase, it will do so only after a series of struggles.

A second and equally daring challenge comes from a plan to reform the party's participation structures by integrating local factions without endangering the party's capacity to act. In the rural areas of Taiwan, the KMT quite often preferred cooperation with local factions to the establishment of a functioning network of party cells. The local party cadres sometimes acted as umpires in the struggle of competing factions, using the party's resources to ensure their cooperation at election time. With shrinking options for patronage and a party organization more sensitive to local influences, new ways have to be found to reflect and integrate the diverging interests of local actors.

Similar problems need to be solved at the national level. Among other improvements, a better integration of the party apparatus and elected politicians in the process of policy formulation is required. At present a policy line is generally formulated and accepted at the top without adequate participation by the elected politicians. Conflicts arising from the efforts of the party apparatus to enforce the official party line and the tactical considerations of candidates trying to increase their election chances are likely to multiply in the future. The present debate concerning the future direction of the KMT's China policy started by the Wisdom Group in the LY parliamentary party may be an indication of what is to come. For tactical reasons, members of this group came out in favour of a 'one China, one Taiwan' policy, disregarding party resolutions and declarations by the chairman stressing the KMT's continued adherence to a one-China policy.

The DPP

The DPP is also challenged by the changing political system, although in a very different way. In the six years following its foundation in the autumn of 1986 the party successfully established itself as the island's major opposition party, at both national and regional levels. But despite a number of spectacular electoral successes the DPP clearly lacks resources. The leadership's hope for a rapid increase in party membership has not materialized. Its present membership of around 70,000 consists mainly of people from the lower middle class and is predominantly Taiwanese, with minimal participation from mainlanders. The party's financial base remains precarious – at one point an imminent threat of insolvency was averted only by a large donation by the then party chairman, Huang Hsin-chieh.

Set up as an association of politicians belonging to the Tangwai and of members of their political staffs, who called themselves 'party workers', the new party immediately confronted a number of problems. Politicians and party workers held conflicting views concerning its character. Supporters looked for a disciplined party dedicated to the realization of its platform, a party in which decisions by the leadership took precedence over the views of individuals in parliament. The majority of the elected politicians, however, hoped for an organization dominated by personalities. Having successfully coped with the limitations imposed upon them by martial law, these politicians wanted an organization that would increase their chances in competition with the KMT.

Inevitably, given the difficulties of uniting a loose opposition movement containing groups with quite different political opinions, and whose main common conviction lay in opposing KMT rule over Taiwan, the party's attempts at integration underwent repeated challenges in subsequent years. Leading members of the early Tangwai movement, who had been sent to gaol following the Kaohsiung incident of 1979, received presidential pardons. They re-entered political life and became influential members of the DPP. More recently an increasing number of prominent members of the Taiwan Independence Movement have returned to the island from the USA. They strengthened the ranks of those groups within the DPP that put the solution of Taiwan's international status above other concerns, and they were instrumental in instigating the increasingly radical declarations of the party on this matter. The various opinion groups within the party have reassembled, establishing several functions whose struggle for influence has become the major cause of intraparty tensions. These groups divide into two overarching organizations, the moderate Formosa Faction (*Meilitao hsi*) and the radical New Tide Faction (*Hsin ch'aoliu hsi*, or HCL), which unite the majority of representatives at times when preparation for important decisions within the party have to be made; only a small number of politicians maintain a neutral position. Both groupings represent complex associations consisting of a core faction and other smaller factions with similar political orientations but tending to operate independently most of the time.

One reason for the continuing competition between the factions can be found in a structure designed to facilitate participation and intraparty democracy at the expense of continuity and efficiency. In order to prevent the development of a dominant party leadership the terms of office of the party Chairman and the Secretary General were limited to a maximum of two years, with re-election prohibited. Members of other leading organizations within the DPP have to stand for re-election after one year. Within the first seven years of its official existence the party had four changes of chairman. The relatively short intervals between elections for the party's leadership guarantee a high level of conflict between its major factions.

The impact of the changing electoral mechanism is felt increasingly by the DPP, as by the KMT, shaping competition between the factions and the electoral strategies of candidates. Even factions such as the HCL, which tends to prioritize the organization and place less importance on acquiring mandates for their members, have been forced to rethink their position in the light of recent developments. In order to maintain their influence within the party as a whole several prominent representatives of the faction that rejected participation in past elections decided to take part in the LY elections of 1992. In preparing for these elections the DPP party leadership encountered problems quite similar to those faced by the KMT: an explosive growth of party members keen to participate in the elections; increasing use of money to influence the electors' decisions; and breaches of party discipline, including participation without prior nomination by the party.

The long-term prospects for the DPP will be influenced mainly by two factors: the intensity of factional conflict and the political priorities set by the party. Both the Tangwai and the DPP in the first years after its establishment gained considerable political support from two groups of voters, whose priorities are not identical: those interested in furthering the Taiwanese cause, and supporters of continuing liberalization and democratization of the political system. Although the DPP considered itself a Taiwanese party from the start, it proved attractive to those parts of the electorate – and political representatives – that were more concerned with political reforms and democratization than with the problem of Taiwan's identity. Over the years demands for Taiwan's independence have increased while toleration of dissenting opinions within the party has decreased. As a result several members in the LY have left the party.

For the time being Taiwanese politics seems to be headed towards a three-party, or alternatively a two-and-a-half party system. The KMT remains the most powerful party, but there is also plenty of room for opposition to grow. Both the DPP in 1993 and the New Party in 1995 have exploited this successfully, to a point where the KMT barely commands a majority in the LY. The electoral mechanism confronts both KMT and DPP with the danger of increasing fragmentation that might lead either to an increase in the number of intraparty factions or to the establishment of new parties by groups of disenchanted party members. The New Party is a graphic illustration of this possibility, which is reinforced by the nature of the presidential system. Executive power rests predominantly in the hands of the president. The government is responsible to him rather than to the LY. Representatives in the LY therefore have less incentive to cooperate with the president, even if they are KMT members. Voting discipline among KMT legislators has been weaker than in other parties. Indeed they may often oppose presidential proposals because they gain more individual publicity by doing so, and such publicity can aid their re-election. Thus the party system remains very fluid.

The political order and national identity

The retirement of the elderly elected representatives and the accession of Taiwanese to the positions of president and party chairman considerably weakened support for two central tenets of the Nationalist regime: the *sunist* nature of the polity enshrined in the constitution formulated by Sun Yat-sen, and the identity of Taiwan as part of China. Both tenets have met with increasing criticism over the years and have been maintained only with great difficulty. At present, however, there are no alternative concepts available that could serve as a basis for a new political outlook acceptable to a majority of the inhabitants of Taiwan.

Since the early 1950s critics of the martial law regime repeatedly argued in favour of restoring constitutional rule based on the constitution of 1946. A similar idea informed the decisions of the Third Plenum of the KMT. This approach, favouring limited constitutional reforms, has become the target of strong criticism in the ensuing debates because the KMT temporized and was unable to formulate a comprehensive policy early in the reform process. The National Affairs Conference convoked by President Lee in June 1990 with the explicit aim of establishing a consensus on the problem of constitutional reform among the diverging opinion groups failed to achieve its task.

In the debate that followed voices opposing a limited reform of the existing constitution and arguing in favour of a new one became more numerous. The advocates of this approach either belonged to the DPP or were politically sympathetic to it. They presented several draft constitutions or outlines of a new basic law which displayed considerable differences both in the norms of the new polity and in its institutional framework relative to the existing constitution. A conference attended by politicians affiliated with the opposition and academics supporting the reform movement deliberated on the outlines of a draft constitution that would combine the different approaches of previous drafts. The conference accepted a draft 'Constitution for Taiwan' which was later incorporated into the political platform of the DPP.

The differences between the present constitution of the Republic and the draft constitution are profound, in terms both of the norms that should guide the polity and of its political institutions. These differences reflect the political outlook of the protagonists in the debate: while the KMT wants to maintain and reaffirm the core values and the institutions of the existing political order, the supporters of the 'Constitution for Taiwan' aim at the creation of a new political order with a different set of values, applicable only to Taiwan and its surrounding islands. In addition to denying any claims beyond the areas currently under the control of the government, the draft constitution also envisages fundamental changes in the basic design of the republic's political institutions. It discards the present division into five powers, opting for a presidential system based on a threefold division of powers.

The debate between the proponents of the two contrasting approaches to the constitutional problem did not achieve any tangible results so far as a reconciliation of the diverging opinions or the formulation of a new consensus shared by a majority of the population are concerned. Quite to the contrary, the debate was highly politicized and was used by the two opposing camps to further causes of more immediate concern to the parties. The high degree of symbolic politics involved in the debates easily gives way to an exchange of polemics. Neither the different set of norms contained in the constitution and draft constitution, nor the merits or deficiencies of the political institutions they define, has been made the subject of disinterested study.

The debate is likely to continue, and to constitute one of the main areas of political contestation after the presidential election in March 1996. If the government and the KMT continue with their present approach to the problem of constitutional reform, avoiding clear-cut propositions and postponing debates within the party and with the supporters of a new constitution for tactical reasons, it is highly unlikely that a new consensus over the norms and institutions of the political order can develop. Should this be the case, a considerable part of the population on Taiwan will continue to harbour doubts about the legitimacy of the existing constitutional order.

Closely related to the problem of a future political order is the question of Taiwan's identity, a topic which has attracted considerable interest. Intensely debated in magazines and books as well as in public meetings, the issue has implications for both the ends and the conduct of Taiwan's foreign policy and its policy towards mainland China.

The debate is characterized by a profusion of conflicting expectations and perceptions. Most of the population display only limited interest in the discussion, since they are largely content with benefits brought by the present state of affairs and oppose any radical changes. But the fact that the debate on identity is conducted primarily by the government and the politically active sections of the population does little to dampen its intensity, a reflection of the commitment of the participating groups and individuals. Though of little practical importance in the short run, the high symbolic value of any change in the official definition of Taiwan's identity, and its long-term implications, provide additional fuel for controversy.

Under these circumstances the task of the government is quite difficult: devising a formula that does not offend the expectations of the main groups involved, Taiwanese and mainlanders, but that allows a high degree of flexibility in Taiwan's foreign and Chinese policies without unduly offending sensitivities in Beijing. In view of the difficulties involved, the government in Taipei has opted for a form of creative ambiguity with a number of reservations that postpone any resolution of the issue far into the future. President Lee Teng-hui is wont to talk of three Chinas, the two that exist at the moment, and the third reunited one, which will exist at some point in the future.

The 'Guidelines for Reunification' adopted by the government describe a free and democratic reunified China, with prosperity for all of it as the objective. The preconditions for achieving this aim are maintaining a 'one-China policy', but also maintaining the security and prosperity of Taiwan. This compromise formulation leaves room for interpretation and for the integration of conflicting expectations; it also creates a constant need for clarification and does not prevent conflicts over its concrete implications in a number of policy areas.

The difficulties involved in harmonizing conflicting political objectives that result from different perceptions of Taiwan's identity with the more down-to-earth demands of interest groups have become obvious in the process of formulating a new approach to Taiwan's relations with mainland China. Before 1987 the situation appeared to be simple and straightforward: Taiwan was considered part of China. No practical problems for the conduct of business arose from this perception because of the all-embracing confrontation between both governments and because the government in Taipei banned contacts, trade and negotiations with the mainland.

Confronted with conflicting expectations, and demands for a new approach in its China policy, the government and the KMT have until now avoided any open and thoroughgoing debate of the problem and opted instead for a piecemeal approach.

The limitations inherent in this approach have become obvious as economic relations between Taiwan and mainland China have intensified. The absence of clearly formulated political and economic objectives on the part of Taiwan means that economic activities are undertaken exclusively by the individual companies involved, with their own expectations of profits the only consideration. Taiwan still lacks a coherent approach that might use its economic strength to improve its position *vis-à-vis* the government in Peking; there is not even a definition of the limits to economic exchanges set by security requirements.

The assumptions that inform the foreign policy of the ROC have also become subject to intense domestic controversy. This ongoing debate is conducted on two different levels. One involves the expectation of the general population that its government should be able to achieve an international position commensurate with Taiwan's economic strength and its ranking as a leading trading nation. On a second level the conflicting perceptions of Taiwan's identity impinge upon the debate. The question is whether the present foreign policy line, stressing substantial relations and double recognition, is most suited to further the global interests of the island in the long term, or whether it should be replaced by a policy that aims at international recognition of Taiwan as an independent entity. Any success or failure in foreign policy is immediately used as an argument to prove the basic soundness or weakness of the approach. For the time being the government's foreign policy has the support of the KMT parliamentary party in the LY.

The balance sheet and future prospects

After decades of authoritarian rule the Republic of China on Taiwan is now in the midst of a transition to a more democratic form of government. The constitutive elements of the old order are in the process of dissolution, and the first outlines of a new institutional framework have taken shape. A successful completion of the transition process cannot be expected in the near future, however.

The realignment of power, from a single person to a collective leadership, has been achieved. Personal rule has been replaced by the rule of institutions. The position of the parliaments, the NA and the LY within the institutional framework of the republic has been strengthened, but a new distribution of power and influence between the various national institutions has not yet been established. The same applies to the distribution of influence among the groups within the KMT, between mainlanders and Taiwanese, and among those representing various societal interests. New rules guiding the struggle for power and political competition are still to be established. There is no new consensus on the norms and shape of Taiwan's political order.

The present phase of political change is the result of reforms initiated by the leadership of the ruling party. But future changes are most likely to be consequences of the final establishment of elections as the sole mechanism for the distribution of power among competing political parties, which will create pressures for further change.

These pressures will be most keenly felt by the political parties, especially the KMT, whose party organization is still geared towards the necessities of controlling political activity instead of facilitating political participation. Too short a time has passed since the first political reforms for any prediction of whether the present electoral system will lead to the development of a two-party system, and whether it will permit the creation of political parties based on the highly disciplined European model or on loosely structured catch-all parties of the US type. The largest party on Taiwan, the KMT, will be confronted with complex problems of structural reform and realignment of influence among its political elites.

Relations within the executive branches, those of the President and the Premier, are likely to become more complicated, as is the relationship between the executive and the legislative branches. Should the constitution remain unchanged so far as the distribution of power between President and Premier is concerned, and should future incumbents succeed in establishing a good working relationship with the LY, the power of the Premier will considerably increase. Both President and Premier will have to give greater consideration to the demands and preferences of the LY. Whether the LY will gain greater influence in the policy-making process or be paralysed by increasing factional in-fighting remains to be seen.

A consensus on the political order may be difficult to achieve. The major opposition party and a considerable part of the population remain opposed to the assumptions underlying the existing political order. In general there is an air of incumbency fatigue about politics in Taiwan. The government and the ruling party shy away from an open discourse and prefer limited changes. However much the KMT may have reformed, it has been in power in Taiwan continuously since 1945. Thus whenever something goes wrong, it is difficult for the buck not to stop ultimately at the party's door. That is especially true of financial scandals – not least because the KMT has made such efforts to win the support of business.[6] Thus the position of the DPP may continue to improve as much because it is a more credible alternative to the KMT as because of specific features of its own programme. It is therefore possible that the DPP will ultimately gain a majority in the LY, even though most of its supporters are not totally committed to what some think is the party's chief distinguishing policy, i.e. independence for Taiwan. Opinion polls suggest that only 15–20 per cent of the population support such a policy. But before that happens it is easier to envisage an LY after the next elections in 1998 in which no party has an absolute majority – one of the biggest tests of a working democracy. If the parties represented there managed to make the legislature work despite the absence of a majority (and despite the occasional physical violence on the floor of the chamber, which has been shown around the world on television), it would be a clear sign of how strongly rooted democracy had become in Taiwan.

Notes

1 Bruce J. Dickson, 'The Adaptability of Leninist Parties: A Comparison of the Chinese Communist Party and the Kuomintang' (PhD dissertation, University of Michigan, 1994), p. 70.

2 Huei En Peng, *T'aiwan fachante chengchih chingchi fenhsi* ['Analysis of Taiwan's Developing Political Economy'] (Taipei: Fengyun lunch'iang ch'upanshe, 1992), p. 147.

3 Julian Baum, 'Cashing In', *Far Eastern Economic Review*, 12 November 1992, pp. 20–22.

4 Simon Long, *China Quarterly*, 129, 1992, pp. 216–18.

5 *Far Eastern Economic Review*, 11 August 1994, pp. 62–5.

6 Yun-han Chu, 'The Realignment of Business–Government Relations and Regime Transition in Taiwan', in Andrew MacIntyre (ed.), *Business and Government in Industrialising Asia* (St Leonards, NSW, Australia: Allen & Unwin, 1994), pp. 113–41.

Chapter 3

The Taiwanese economy in the 1980s and 1990s

Peter Ferdinand

Introduction

Since 1949 the Taiwanese economy has been among the fastest growing in the world. Between 1953 and 1989 it grew at an annual rate of 8.9 per cent, more than double the average for developing nations (4.71 per cent) and industrialized nations (3.8 per cent). By 1993 its per capita GNP was US$10,852 – the fourth highest in Asia, after Japan, Singapore and Hong Kong, and almost 50 per cent higher than that of the other 'tiger' economy, South Korea. It was nearly three times that of Mexico, which has the highest per capita GNP in Latin America, and it was not far behind those of Ireland, Spain and New Zealand.

It is true that Taiwan is in the region of the world that has seen the highest growth rate since the Second World War, and it has benefited from this regional achievement. Nevertheless according to World Bank statistics, its record over the period 1960-85 was the best in the world after Botswana.[1] It had the highest growth rate in East Asia, higher even than Japan's. Whereas Japan's period of roughly 10 per cent annual growth lasted for 15 years, between 1955 and 1970, Taiwan has maintained this momentum for almost 40 years. Indeed, according to the *Far Eastern Economic Review*, its average annual GDP growth rate over the period 1980–92 was 10.6 per cent, the highest in Asia and higher than the 9.1 per cent averaged by the People's Republic of China, which is much better known for its success.[2] This has been a startling performance for a state which at the outset seemed unlikely to survive invasion from the mainland, and which had a primarily agricultural economy endowed with few natural resources.

Over the whole of this period the economy went through progressive

Table 3.1 Sectoral composition of GDP (%)

Year	Agriculture	Industry	Services
1952	32.2	19.7	48.1
1962	23.8	24.2	52.0
1972	12.6	38.9	48.5
1982	6.8	44.4	48.8
1992	3.5	40.1	56.4
1994	3.1	39.0	57.9

Source: *Industry of Free China*, June 1995, p. 51.

Table 3.2 Sectoral distribution of labour (%)

Year	Agriculture	Industry	Services
1952	56.1	16.9	27.0
1962	49.7	21.0	29.3
1972	33.0	31.8	35.2
1982	18.9	41.3	39.8
1992	12.3	39.6	48.1
1994	10.9	39.2	49.9

Source: *Industry of Free China*, June 1995, p. 55.

stages of quite rapid industrialization, with the result that Taiwan has now become a developed industrial nation (see Table 3.1). This has been paralleled by a shift in the structure of employment away from agriculture, first into industry and then, more recently, into services (see Table 3.2).

Taiwanese society has become predominantly urban, with the shift in popular tastes that normally accompanies urbanization. The process has been rapid, and the development of infrastructure has lagged behind, a burden borne by consumers and town-dwellers. Their cumulative discontent has been one of the factors underlying the erosion of support for the KMT since the late 1980s, once the process of democratization got under way.

Economic policy to the 1980s

1949–60

The first four years after the Republic of China was forced to move to Taiwan were devoted to restoring normality to the economy, bringing down inflation from the astronomic levels reached in the last years of the Nationalist regime on the mainland while committing as many resources as possible to guard against an imminently expected invasion. Nevertheless the state launched a key policy – land reform – which was to lay the foundation both for subsequent economic growth and for the high degree of economic equality that was achieved at the same time.

Land reform had always figured among the goals of the Nationalist government on the mainland, but prior to the Second World War it had not been carried out for two basic reasons. First, there was opposition from local elites, upon whose support and cooperation the government depended. Secondly, land reform was a basic objective of the Chinese Communist Party, so some KMT supporters regarded it as 'subversive' and wanted to distance the party from it.

When the Nationalist leadership returned to Taiwan after the Second World War, however, it was much less close to the local elites on the island. The KMT suspected it of having collaborated with the Japanese colonizers and therefore of being less than wholeheartedly patriotic. The local landlord elites, on the other hand, resented the heavy-handed efforts of KMT officials and carpet-baggers to take control of the island and its economy. As mentioned in Chapter 2, the riots that started on 28 February 1947 and that were suppressed with the loss of thousands of lives created a divide between 'Taiwanese' and 'mainlanders' which in a sense 'freed' the Nationalist authorities from the need to defer to the concerns of local elites. Land reform, therefore, could be put back on the political agenda. For the leadership what counted was the fact that reform would weaken the power and potential opposition of local elites. Thus it was a vital step for the Nationalists in ensuring their political control of the island.

The policy was implemented between 1949 and 1953. It led to the increased dependence of the former landlords upon the state, since they were reimbursed for their land with commodity bonds paying only 4 per cent interest and shares in four state companies, the value of which was at the state's disposal. And it also created a much larger class of peasant farmers who were grateful to the state for the land they had been granted. Between 1949 and 1957 the proportion of owner-farmers in the agricultural population as a whole rose from 38 to 60 per cent.[3] Since at that time the overwhelming majority of the population was still rural, the government's domestic legitimacy was greatly increased. Equally importantly, however, it altered the terms of trade between industry and agriculture, so that some resources could be redirected away from agriculture and rural society towards the industrialization effort which was about to get under way.

From 1953 the government introduced a series of four-year national plans, which were intended to provide direction for the industrialization of a country with still very limited national resources, especially foreign exchange.[4] Until 1960 the chief priority was encouraging concentration upon import substitution and the domestic market. In this it was following the conventional wisdom of the time on economic development. The result was an average annual growth rate of 7.6 per cent, which was among the highest in the world at that time, although the 1950s subsequently proved to be the period of Taiwan's lowest growth rate.

1960–73
By 1960 the Taiwanese economy had already encountered the difficulty of creating a modern industry of adequate size with a population of around 10 million. In addition the government was concerned about a shortage of foreign currency to pay for the import of all the equipment needed for industrialization, as well as the strong possibility that US aid – then running at around $100 million per year – would soon be ended. So it decided upon a drastic change of course. With US advice, it opted for a strategy of exports to maintain growth. At the same time, as growth began to bring a little prosperity to the population, it took measures to encourage savings and investment. Between 1961 and 1972 average annual growth rose to 10.3 per cent. Industrial products overtook and left far behind agricultural products in terms of share of exports. Whereas in 1960 industry provided 32.3 per cent of exports, in 1970 the comparable figure was 78.6 per cent. It was in this decade that Taiwan began to make a mark upon international markets.

1973–83
Between 1973 and 1983 economic growth increased even more, on average to 12.8 per cent per year. As Japanese economic growth began to fall back towards only half that level, Taiwan was attracting international attention for its performance. This was impressive despite two major oil crises, which hit Taiwan both directly, because of its own dependence upon oil for energy, and indirectly because of the impact of the crises on other countries which therefore had less money to buy Taiwanese exports. In 1974 growth plummeted to 1.2 per cent, and the government introduced change in domestic policy. Domestic growth was now stimulated through increased programmes of public works spending to counter

the effect of international setbacks. By so doing the government moved towards synthesizing the characteristics of the two preceding periods, which had given priority first to import substitution and then to exports.

The Taiwanese economy in the 1980s: crisis, triumph, puzzlement

For the Taiwanese government, the decade began in crisis and ended in puzzlement. In between, however, came almost a decade of continuing success, marked by three great triumphs: the rapid overcoming of the oil crisis of 1979–80, the maintenance of rapid growth despite diplomatic derecognition by the USA, and the surge in exports in the second half of the decade.

The years 1979–80 were particularly difficult, even traumatic, for Taiwan. In addition to the US abrogation of its treaty commitments to the ROC, there came the second round of sudden oil-price rises. For a country which was entirely dependent upon the outside world for oil and therefore for almost all of its electricity, this was potentially as great a blow to the economy as the oil-price rises of 1973 had been.

Yet the regime quickly recovered its composure. 'Abandonment' by the USA did not lead to invasion – indeed, as we shall see in Chapter 4, by the early 1990s the ROC was bidding to rejoin international organizations. The basis of this self-confidence was the economic achievement of the 1980s.

In 1981 economic growth fell to 6.2 per cent, and in 1982 to 3.6 per cent. The rate then improved again, with almost 9 per cent in 1983 and 11.6 per cent in 1986. Throughout the 1980s the economy achieved an average growth rate of 8.25 per cent (see Table 3.3).

Table 3.3 Annual economic growth rate

Year	%	Year	%
1979	8.2	1987	12.7
1980	7.3	1988	7.8
1981	6.2	1989	8.2
1982	3.6	1990	5.4
1983	8.5	1991	7.6
1984	10.6	1992	6.8
1985	5.0	1993	6.3
1986	11.6	1994	6.5

Source: *Industry of Free China*, June 1995, p. 66.

As it happened, the oil-price shock of 1979 came almost at the end of a phase of economic development on Taiwan that had concentrated on export promotion, combined with some measures for import substitution. The effect had been to strengthen the domestic economy so that it could compete internationally. Indeed it was largely as a result of increased exports to the USA that Taiwan was able to weather the oil-price rise so successfully. It had become a modern, internationally competitive, industrial economy.

The government was then confronted by a new set of problems of adaptation. 'By 1983 [the government of Taiwan] could take on an entirely new and unprecedentedly ideological appeal by accepting the principle of the survival of the fittest and the discipline of international competition in the domestic market – a far cry from the xenophobia and autarkic appeal of the early import substitution era.'[5] It was a paradox of the 1980s that at a time of significant uncertainty about the security situation of the ROC, the regime began to open up the economy to the outside world as never before.

By the end of the decade Taiwan's export/GDP ratio for goods, which had fluctuated between 40 and 50 per cent throughout the 1980s, had stabilized at just over 40 per cent. In the 1950s it had been around 10 per cent.

All these economic successes, however, failed to bring the nation the freedom of manoeuvre to solve the problems accumulated from earlier phases of development, and a sense of puzzlement set in. Some of the problems came to be seen as too complex to be solved simply by throwing money at them. And the inability to solve them followed also from the greater difficulty the government experienced in trying to direct the economy by using ever less direct methods and relying instead on markets.

Compounding the sense of puzzlement was the unexpected eruption of social instability. The export successes which had brought considerable extra wealth to the country also brought inflation, especially in land prices, and gambling fever. A game called *ta chia le* ('everyone happy'), which involved betting on daily movements of the stock exchange index, swept the nation. The abolition of martial law led to a dramatic upsurge in industrial unrest, with large numbers of strikes. It also led to an upsurge of crime. In 1991 reported crime, which had remained static for several years, suddenly shot up by 30 per cent, largely because of dramatically increased prosecutions for gambling and drunkenness. Greater prosperity seemed to have created greater social turmoil.

The domestic economy

Towards the end of the 1980s, new problems were beginning to appear. The surge in income resulting from exports combined with the relatively underdeveloped financial sector meant that there were few opportunities for investment on Taiwan – and until 1988 it was difficult for individuals to invest overseas. So loose money fuelled a dramatic increase in land prices as people sought stability for their investments in land ownership, and also spectacular gyrations on the stock market. In turn all this led to a reversal of the earlier trend towards income equalization. As a result the Taiwanese authorities concentrated on the need to deepen the financial services sector, so that individuals would be able to invest more, and more safely, in a variety of sources.

Although the official ideology of the regime remained overwhelmingly oriented towards serving the needs of industry, with little sympathy either for the role of finance capital or for finance capitalists, it acknowledged that the very lack of a substantial financial services sector was hurting industry. So in 1988 the first of a series of measures were taken to liberalize financial markets. Later, in the early 1990s, private banks were legalized, with 15 new ones approved.

In addition to the rapid growth of the economy, the relatively even distribution of national income across the population was especially noteworthy. In the initial phases of industrialization, economies tend to widen income disparities, although economic-development theory expects that these will flatten out later to some extent. In the case of Taiwan, however, income distribution was relatively little disturbed by the industrialization drive of the 1960s and 1970s. In fact the 1970s saw a significant increase in income equality, as measured by the ratio of the income of the top fifth of the population to that of the bottom fifth. This ratio had been 5.25 in 1966 and 5.28 in 1968, but in 1970 it fell to 4.58, reaching its lowest point of 4.18 in 1978 – one of the lowest ratios in the world.

The main reason for this was the land reform programme of the early 1950s, which significantly reduced the wealth of the former landed elite on the island. In the 1960s and 1970s, however, new factors restrained the pressures which in other economies widened income disparities. Some depended on the government. One obvious factor was the state's control over trade unions, which kept labour demands moderate, and martial law prevented large-scale strikes. In addition, government policies aimed at encouraging labour-intensive industries soaked up less productive rural labour.

The structural characteristics of Taiwanese society were also important. Compared with other economies the Taiwanese industrial structure has been marked by a predominance of small and medium-sized companies, i.e. manufacturing and construction companies with assets of not more than NT$120 million and sales of not more than NT$40 million (i.e. roughly US$5 million and US$2 million respectively). The economy sustains a pronounced entrepreneurial ethos, which encourages individuals to leave existing companies and form their own so as to develop new ideas. The constant influx of industrial capital from newcomers led to a dispersal rather than a concentration of income. Another factor in keeping incomes relatively even was the raising of levels of education. Here the Confucian tradition contributed, with families placing a very high priority on education of the young and making sacrifices for the sake of it, and then expecting their children to share the benefits among the family.

Government welfare programmes did not play an important role in achieving this relative equality. Almost all support for dependents remained the responsibility of individuals and their families. In turn this contributed to economic development as individuals chose to save a surprisingly high proportion of their income, as an insurance against misfortune. Indeed it is striking that as the Taiwanese economy has grown, so too has people's readiness to save, particularly since until the late 1980s state banks offered very low rates of interest for depositors. In 1952 gross savings represented 15.3 per cent of GNP, and the proportion has risen steadily since 1957. Since 1970 annual gross savings in the economy have averaged over 30 per cent, and in all years but three they have exceeded gross investment; in 1985 they were more than double. This was not just due to individual savers. In part it reflected the enormous increase in Taiwan's exports in that year, since it is a consequence of international accounting practices that trade surpluses are counted as national savings. Nevertheless private savings remained at a very high level.

One major section of Taiwanese society felt disadvantaged by the upsurge in national wealth in the 1980s: the farmers. Whereas in the 1950s they had benefited from the land reform programme, they had felt since then that the terms of trade had moved against them. This was especially true in the late 1960s, as industry lured more people to the cities and caused agricultural labour rates to rise. From the early 1970s the government initiated policies which fixed a floor support price for rice above the assumed production cost. By the early 1990s it was calculated that this subsidy was costing the government an annual US$2–3 billion. From the viewpoint of the government it was aggravating, too, because it kept out cheaper foreign rice and so created additional trade disputes, especially with the USA. As a result, in the 1980s the government began to encourage farmers to diversify their crops and to enlarge the size of land holdings.[6]

Foreign trade

During the 1980s Taiwan's foreign trade policies reaped their greatest successes (see Table 3.4). Above all this success was achieved in US markets, where gains in the first half of the 1980s were reinforced by the Plaza Accords between the G5 countries to manage the devaluation of the US dollar and the revaluation of the yen. US importers turned to both South Korea and Taiwan for alternative sources of supply. The result was that Taiwan's exports to the USA soared from US$30.7 billion in 1985 to reach $53.7 billion in 1987 and $66.3 billion in 1989, more than doubling in four years. In the peak year 1987, the trade surplus with the USA amounted to US$16 billion, i.e. 86 per cent of Taiwan's total trade surplus. The profits that followed from these additional exports were then sometimes reinvested in US companies by Taiwanese companies flush with cash; the subsequent performance of these investments was not, however, always satisfactory.

The trade surplus aroused official US concern and focused attention on Taiwan's foreign trade policies and infringements of intellectual property law. The old readiness on the part of the USA to tolerate a

Table 3.4 Foreign trade surpluses

Year	US$m	Year	US$m
1980	78	1988	10,929
1981	1,411	1989	14,039
1982	3,316	1990	12,499
1983	4,836	1991	13,318
1984	8,497	1992	9,464
1985	10,624	1993	8,030
1986	15,684	1994	7,700
1987	18,655		

Sources: *Taiwan Statistical Data Book* (Taipei: Council for Economic Planning and Development, 1989); *Monthly Bulletin of Statistics of the Republic of China* (Directorate-General of Budget, Accounting and Statistics, May 1995).

Table 3.5 Regional destinations of Taiwanese exports (%)

Year	Japan	USA	Hong Kong	Europe	Others
1952	52.6	3.5	7.7	5.3	30.9
1960	37.7	11.5	12.6	6.0	32.2
1970	14.6	38.1	9.2	10.1	28.0
1980	11.0	34.1	7.8	11.6	35.5
1985	11.3	48.1	8.3	9.8	22.5
1990	12.4	32.4	12.7	18.2	24.3
1994	11.0	26.2	22.7	13.9	26.2

Source: *Taiwan Statistical Data Book* (Taipei: Council for Economic Planning and Development, 1995).

biased foreign trade regime so as to avoid having to subsidize Taiwan for defence reasons was gradually undermined as the cumulative cost in US jobs became politically more significant. The US administration began to subject Taiwan to the same kind of pressure that had previously been directed at Japan. By the early 1990s Taiwan had been officially listed by the USA as the state most guilty of infringements of intellectual property rights.

This had an effect. The Taiwanese government responded by encouraging businesses to look for alternative markets. Initially Europe was preferred. With trade also went investment, as Taiwanese companies worried that the Single European Market might lead to barriers against exports from other parts of the world. Increased trade followed, with Hong Kong and, indirectly, with the mainland. In 1992 Taiwanese exports to Hong Kong surpassed those to Europe, and the gap has continued to grow (see Table 3.5).

Taiwanese imports have also shown significant geographical shifts, as can be seen from Table 3.6. Whereas for roughly its first 15 years Taiwan exported to pay for imports from the USA, from the 1970s it needed to export to the rest of the world, and primarily the USA, to pay for imports from Japan. Japan has continued to be the biggest exporter to Taiwan, even though the Taiwanese government introduced some restrictions. Japanese-made cars, for instance, cannot be imported, and Japanese car companies have to assemble cars on the island with Taiwanese partners. The structure of Japanese imports has changed fundamentally since the 1950s. Initially they consisted of primary products, but increasingly manufactured goods have taken over. Many Taiwanese companies, e.g. in electronics and information technology, are still extremely dependent

Table 3.6 Sources of Taiwanese imports by region (%)

Year	Japan	USA	Hong Kong	Europe	Others
1952	31.2	45.7	9.0	6.6	16.5
1960	35.3	38.1	1.6	11.2	15.4
1970	42.8	23.9	1.8	9.7	23.6
1980	27.1	23.7	1.3	9.4	39.8
1985	27.6	23.6	1.6	12.2	36.6
1990	29.2	23.0	2.7	17.5	30.3
1994	29.0	21.1	1.8	18.7	29.4

Source: *Taiwan Statistical Data Book* (Taipei: Council for Economic Planning and Development, 1995).

upon supplies of high-quality components from Japan. More recently, with increasing prosperity, Taiwanese consumer tastes have become more sophisticated, and European exports to Taiwan have grown significantly. In addition, at the end of the 1980s the Taiwanese government initiated a five-year 'Little Europe' programme to encourage European manufacturers with international brand names, such as Benetton, Pierre Cardin, Pierre Balmain and Stylo, to manufacture products in Taiwan for the Japanese.

What is clear from Tables 3.5 and 3.6 is that Taiwan continues to need to export to the USA and, increasingly, to China in order to pay for its imports from Japan and, to a lesser extent, from Europe, not to mention oil from the Middle East. In 1994 Taiwan's trade surplus with the mainland was roughly equal to its overall trade surplus. In practice, exports to China are often processed there for re-export to the USA. In that sense Taiwan is for the moment still dependent upon the US market, although less directly.

Problems for the 1990s

By the end of the 1980s the Taiwanese economy had reached another turning point. At the middle of the decade the domestic sector accounted for about two-fifths of total real economic growth. But by 1991 it was accounting for all economic growth, as imports were beginning to grow, however slightly, faster than exports.[7]

This reorientation pleased the government. Like the deficit with Japan, the Taiwanese trade surplus with the USA remained stubborn. Major efforts at export diversification had been made, with the effect that whereas in 1987 the USA was still taking 40 per cent of ROC exports, by 1991 this had fallen to 28.5 per cent, but Taiwan's trade surplus with the USA was still $8.2 billion. So domestic-led expansion, which could lead to greater imports, fitted in with the new mood in Washington.

By the end of the decade, too, pressure was increasing for the government to pay more attention to the domestic economy, and also to the environment. The overworked infrastructure, especially in Taipei, took its toll on the energies of its still growing population. Environmental pollution, too, was an increasing source of concern. Tales of infringements of the law by business occurred more frequently in the press. And as the regime began to achieve levels of per capita income which allowed the World Bank to classify it as a 'high-income country', ordinary people began to feel that they were entitled to greater and more tangible rewards for all their efforts. More importantly, in a regime undergoing democratization, the KMT leadership and the government were increasingly aware of the need to pay more attention to public opinion.

All of this led the government to introduce a massive Six-Year Development Programme in 1990, which was intended both to create the R&D basis for an advanced industrial economy which could compete internationally, and to remedy the perceived bottlenecks and shortages in the domestic economy.

The overall stated aim was to raise the per capita GNP from just under US$8,000 in 1990 to $14,000 in 1996, which would give the ROC the twentieth highest per capita GNP in the world. According to the plan, the state would focus its attention on developing ten major emerging industries and eight key technologies. The new key industries are telecommunications, information, consumer electronics, semiconductors, precision machinery and automation, aerospace, advanced materials, speciality chemicals and pharmaceuticals, medical and health care, and pollution control. The new key technologies are opto-electronics, computer software, industrial automation, materials applications, advanced sensing technology, biotechnology, resources development and energy conservation.

In addition to these measures to strengthen industry and its physical infrastructure, the plan made commitments to improve the quality of life in terms of social services, notably to provide national health insurance in 1994, and also to make more resources available for the care of the aged. More would also be done to improve the quality of the air, and to reduce other forms of environmental pollution.

The total cost of all these measures was put at US$300 billion, i.e. roughly double the island's GDP. In 1994, however, the government was forced to cut the programme by a fifth, as it became clear that it had overreached itself. Moreover, the Legislative Yuan was withholding support for the financing of one of the showpiece projects, the high-speed rail link between Taipei and Kaohsiung.

The Six-Year Programme has been a moderate success, and the target for per capita GDP income to reach $14,000 by 1996 is almost on course. In 1994 the figure achieved was $11,600. Nevertheless the vicissitudes of the plan are further reminders of the increasing policy complexities with which the Taiwanese government is having to grapple because of, as much as despite, previous economic success.

Attempts to assess Taiwan's future economic performance need to take account not only of the system's past successes but also of the policy issues it will have to resolve if it is going to sustain the previous rate of growth. The next sections will consider a number of these issues.

Industry

Although it is projected that agriculture will represent an even smaller share of GNP in 1996 (2.8 per cent, as compared with 4.3 per cent in 1990), further gains in economic growth cannot be made by increasing the numbers of people employed in more productive sectors such as industry. There are no longer significant numbers of people left working the land who can move to industry and throughout the 1980s the proportion of the population aged over 15 in employment remained stable at around 60 per cent. Instead Taiwanese industry will be expected to aim for growth through concentration on capital- and technology-intensive methods.

Partly as a result of full employment, labour costs have been rising. In the 1980s they grew at an average rate of 6.4 per cent, faster than in all the G7 countries except Japan, where the rate was 6.6 per cent. This pressure of labour costs has encouraged Taiwanese firms to think increasingly of locating factories abroad. On the other hand, as of 1990, hourly compensation costs for production workers in manufacturing in Taiwan were only a fifth of those in the USA and Germany, and a quarter of those of all the other G7 countries except for the UK.[8] Thus from a global perspective, Taiwanese industry as a whole remained internationally competitive. In Pacific Asia, however, where wage costs are even lower, Taiwan faces a stiffer challenge.

It is also worth remembering that although Taiwanese electronics and clothing products have dominated the attention of foreign assessments of the industrial structure of Taiwan, heavy industry has been taking an increasing share of overall industrial output: 63.3 per cent in 1994, compared with 31.1 per cent in 1961.[9] A large part of this increase is represented by growth in the chemicals sector. Another important development has been the growth of industries producing communications, electronics and transport equipment, which now constitute the core of Taiwanese manufactured exports. But state-owned, defence-related industries are also extremely important. In the 1970s and 1980s the government promoted the development of large public enterprises such as the China Petroleum Corporation and the China Steel Corporation, partly as a way of developing economies of scale, although these companies often enjoyed close links with other enterprises associated with the KMT. Since the 1980s rival companies have grown up and have now become more ready to assert their own rights as well as to contest the privileges of companies run by the state or the ruling party. Some of the state-owned heavy industrial companies have been or will be privatized, so that the state's role in them will change, but it seems extremely unlikely that they will be allowed to close, at least as long as a significant defence need remains. The problem of reducing the drag that they exercise on the economy will persist.

During the 1980s it became more widely recognized that state support for individual industries, whether or not they were dominated by state-owned enterprises, would not necessarily result in strong, healthy companies. The car industry in Taiwan is a case in point. The state has banned direct imports of cars manufactured in Japan. This led the major Japanese car-makers to assemble models in partnership with local companies. The result has not, however, been a strong domestic car industry. Car-makers have remained heavily dependent upon Japanese designs and technology. If and when Taiwan enters the World Trade Organization, these restrictions on Japanese imports will have to be phased out, in which case most local manufacturers will be put out of business. The Taiwanese government has tacitly accepted that this will happen, and is now trying to make the best of past efforts by building up Taiwanese car-component manufacturers so that they can become suppliers for multinational corporations.

R&D

Despite all its successes Taiwanese industry is still exercised by a structural problem which has scarcely changed over the past forty years, namely the size of enterprises. As already mentioned, most enterprises are small or medium-sized. They have been extremely nimble in finding new niches in which to operate, both at home and abroad, but they find it difficult to engage in R&D activities because of the costs involved. They also find it difficult to provide adequate specialized training for their employees. Insofar as scientific and technological innovation is likely to become an increasingly important element in international competitiveness, these are obvious weaknesses. Expenditure on civilian R&D in Taiwan as a proportion of GNP is less than half that of Japan or the USA,[10] and the state plans to remedy this disparity by organizing R&D in its own science parks, such as the one at Hsinchu. It plans to establish between 20 and 30 intelligence industrial parks by the year 2005.

Yet a number of factors could work in Taiwan's favour. First there is the very large number of Taiwanese scientists who went abroad for graduate study and never returned. Between 1951 and 1988 slightly more than 90 per cent of the students who went abroad to study, mostly in the USA, stayed there.[11] The government has made great efforts to track these people down and entice them back. One factor on its side is that salaries in Taiwan for those with PhDs are now comparable to those in California. Another attraction is democratization and the opening up of public life. Taiwan no longer seems so qualitatively different in these respects from the much more open society of the USA to which Taiwanese abroad have become accustomed. Significant numbers have returned, and this has been reflected in the increasing technological sophistication of Taiwanese computer firms, many having reached state-of-the-art manufacture. The contacts returning engineers still have with Silicon Valley in California allow these firms to remain at the forefront of technological development. They have certainly become a challenge for Japan.[12] On the other hand, it remains to be seen whether other sectors of Taiwanese industry will be able to achieve and maintain a similar rate of technological innovation.

Another factor in Taiwan's favour is the increasing tendency of companies in high-technology industries to form partnerships to develop new technologies rather than going it alone. This is true even of the largest multinationals. In such a climate smaller companies with valuable technological strengths may be able to take part in a burgeoning industry by forming joint ventures. This fact, combined with the effects of the rise in the value of the yen, has indeed led Japanese corporations to collaborate with Taiwanese computer-component manufacturers.

But at the same time, the problem of attitudes among Taiwanese business people remains. Typically accustomed to running family firms where their overriding concern is profits at the end of the current year, many have not yet adapted their attitudes to managing technologically more sophisticated companies, where the returns on investment are much more long-term.

The government will continue to highlight the ten 'emerging industries' and eight key technologies identified by the Six-Year Development Programme. It will also need to retain its industrial capability which is greater than those of its city-state entrepôt rivals Hong Kong and Singapore. This strength is partly explained by the fact that the Taiwanese economy is significantly larger than those of its rivals among the newly industrializing economies (NIEs). But it is also connected to the security needs of the regime. Indeed as the ROC now has no security alliance with another country, the need for self-reliance in defence capability will remain a primary concern. One sign of this is the strong interest Taiwan shows in the aerospace industry, even if recent deals with McDonnell Douglas and British Aerospace have fallen through.

Service sector and infrastructure

Until recently the service sector received only residual government attention, since the primary national focus was on export of goods. And it should be noted that manufacturing industry still accounts for a higher proportion of GDP than is the average for both industrializing and industrialized nations, while services constitute a relatively smaller proportion. In the late 1980s the share of industry in GDP was 44 per cent for Taiwan, 39 per cent for middle-income developing economies, 36 per cent for low-income developing economies and 34 per cent for developed ones.[13]

Attention is now shifting to a better and fuller supply of services and more domestic-led growth. Partly this is because of the legacy of neglected public services and environmental pollution from the era of high-speed industrial growth – citizens increasingly expect improvements in their standards of living to match the development successes.

It is partly, too, because inadequate services may hold back industry. The underdeveloped financial services sector, for example, has made the task of raising capital more difficult than in rival countries. Moreover, the relative shallowness of that sector, and the lack of diversified investment opportunities encouraged people – assuming they needed such encouragement – to gamble with money rather than invest it, especially in the heady days of export successes in the late 1980s.

Consequently another goal of the Six-Year Programme is to increase the range of available financial services. The ultimate aim is to turn Taipei into a regional financial-services centre. This involves six targets. First, the development of the foreign-exchange market would be integrated with that of the offshore banking unit and the foreign-currency market. The next two targets would be the creation of a derivatives market and a gold market. Fourthly, the bond and securities markets would be expanded and internationalized. Fifthly, the stock market would be strengthened and also internationalized; and finally, the insurance market would be developed and opened. Originally a target date of 1996 was set – one year before the return of Hong Kong to the PRC. Were that transfer to go badly, Taipei might be ready to pick up some of the pieces.

Recent official estimates have suggested that Taiwan would be halfway to achieving the second, third and sixth targets and three-quarters of the way to achieving the rest by the year 2005.[14] Nevertheless it is difficult to envisage that Taiwan would ever be able to take over all the international financial functions performed by Hong Kong, even if the handover to China were to go very badly wrong. Other countries and cities in the region, including Singapore and Malaysia, are also aiming at developing business of this kind. And for Taiwan it would require a dramatic liberalization of financial regulation and of the economy as a whole, at a time when the risks of dramatic fluctuations in, say, foreign capital and exchange rates could be devastating for Taiwanese industry. Taiwan needs to retain a significant industrial base, whereas Hong Kong does not.

The collapse of the Mexican economy at the end of 1994 was a salutary lesson about the risks of miscalculation in opening up an economy, and for Taiwan it was a very pertinent one since in gross terms the Mexican economy was slightly larger than that of Taiwan, with a currency backed by oil reserves, unlike Taiwan's. Yet Mexico was still forced to turn to the USA for help. Would the USA be so ready to bail out Taiwan? Even if Taiwan has the second largest foreign reserves in the world – over US$100 billion – would this be enough to prevent speculation against the NT dollar, considering that even the European Community was unable to prevent speculators driving the pound and the lira out of the Exchange Rate Mechanism? Would the ROC government be willing to open up its economy fully even if it meant that a rapidly growing PRC could speculate against it? The most that seems likely is that Taiwan will become a more serious competitor to Singapore in offering international financial services. But that will still mark a significant widening of the services on offer.

In the early 1990s the Taiwanese government outlined plans to turn the island into an Asia-Pacific Operations Centre, targeting non-Asian multinationals which might appreciate a partner that could assist with trade deals with the rest of East Asia. By spring 1993 a number of multinationals, such as AT&T, ICI, Philips, Federal Express, Bayer, Glaxo, Ciba Vision, Microsoft and DEC had all opened regional centres on Taiwan.

However, this policy has major cost implications for Taiwan: it will involve upgrading airport and port facilities and high-technology industries, as well as creating financial, telecommunications and media centres. The government, with a goal of achieving an 'efficient division of labour between Taiwan, the Chinese mainland and southeast Asian nations',[15] in many ways seems to be aiming to repeat the evolution of Hong Kong, which in the 1980s had exported a large part of its labour-intensive, low-wage manufacturing to mainland China, while the colony itself concentrated upon higher-value services and skills. As a strategy for strengthening Taiwan's economic links with its neighbours, it makes a great deal of sense. Yet the ability to achieve all these goals ultimately depends on a high degree of cooperation with the mainland, and that is not something that Taiwan controls.

Foreign trade and investment abroad

As Taiwan has reached full employment, and as other costs of production on Taiwan have risen (for example, in the late 1980s some land prices rose thirty-fold), many manufacturing companies have sought to invest overseas in lower-cost countries to preserve market share internationally. This means that over the next decade Taiwan will become a mature investing country, with a significant proportion of national income coming from repatriated profits.

The main thrust of Taiwan's trade and foreign investment policy will continue to be diversification. Both its experience of trade frictions with the USA, and its security aims of trying to maximize its freedom of manoeuvre without becoming too dependent upon any one country for support, will ensure that Taiwan and its businesses will search out new trade partners. For example, Europe's share of Taiwan's exports rose from 14.7 per cent in 1987 to 18.4 per cent in 1991; and over the past few years about 400 Taiwanese companies have set up operations in South Africa.

But it is above all in the Asia-Pacific region that Taiwan's trade and investment efforts are likely to be felt. According to the Ministry of Economic Affairs in Taipei, Taiwanese companies invested roughly US$12 billion in Southeast Asia between 1987 and 1992, which represented about half of all capital outflows from Taiwan over that period.[16] They were attracted by stable governments, natural resources, relatively low wage rates and increasingly affluent consumers, not to mention the significant overseas Chinese communities. And they were also drawn to being part of the most dynamic region in the world economy. Even in Vietnam, Taiwan is now the largest foreign investor, and the government in Taipei has encouraged firms to go there as an alternative to the PRC. In fact there is increasing speculation that in the next few years Taiwanese entrepreneurs will pay less attention to Southeast Asia and concentrate instead on developing investments in Vietnam and mainland China.

The most dramatic development in the region has been the rise in Taiwanese trade with and investment in the mainland. Since trade still cannot take place directly between the two sides, usually going via Hong Kong, and since investment on the mainland is still technically illegal for Taiwanese companies, these changes are remarkable. There are no precise figures either for trade or for investment, but Hong Kong government statistics on trade between Taiwan and the mainland passing through the colony are reckoned to give a fairly accurate picture (see Table 3.7).

In current-value terms, therefore, Taiwanese indirect exports to the PRC via Hong Kong alone have risen almost 400 times since the PRC began to open up to the outside world, while PRC exports to Taiwan have risen 23 times.

As for Taiwanese investments on the mainland, in March 1993 the Central Bank of China on Taiwan estimated that Taiwan's net capital investments on the mainland totalled US$6 billion in 1991–2, i.e. 45 per cent of all Taiwanese foreign investment in that period.[17] More recently the PRC, which has an interest in maximizing the apparent scale of Taiwanese investments on the mainland, claimed that the figure was $22 billion, making Taiwan the second largest overseas investor there.[18]

The Taiwanese government remains nervous about the scale of these activities, fearing that they might later be used by Peking to put pressure on the ROC in negotiations. Some of the larger companies, too, are for the moment reluctant to invest in long-term capital-intensive projects on the mainland for fear of political instability. For the first few years, the

55

Table 3.7 Indirect trade between Taiwan and the PRC via Hong Kong (million US$)

	Total trade	Exports to PRC	Imports from PRC	Trade balance
1979	77.76	21.47	56.29	-34.82
1980	311.18	234.97	76.21	158.76
1981	459.33	384.15	75.18	308.97
1982	278.47	194.45	84.02	110.43
1983	247.69	157.84	89.85	67.99
1984	553.20	425.45	127.75	297.70
1985	1102.73	986.83	115.90	870.93
1986	955.55	811.33	144.22	667.11
1987	1515.47	1226.53	288.94	937.59
1988	2720.91	2242.22	478.69	1763.53
1989	3483.39	2896.49	586.90	2309.59
1990	4043.62	3278.26	765.36	2512.90
1991	5793.11	4667.15	1125.95	3541.20
1992	7406.90	6287.93	1118.97	5168.96
1993	8688.98	7585.42	1103.35	6481.86
1994	9809.50	8517.20	1292.30	7224.90

Source: *Transfer Trade Statistics* (Statistics Department, Hong Kong Government, 1995).

investments were small-scale, often with machinery which had already been written off by their Taiwanese owners, so that any output and profit was almost literally money for nothing. Since 1993, however, an increasing number of larger companies have begun to invest there as well. Now 70 companies listed on the Taipei Stock Exchange – one-fifth of the total – have invested in the mainland, although they too have kept the scale of individual investments small, presumably to minimize the impact of something going wrong.[19]

Yet the government cannot be entirely unhappy with these developments. The companies making the investments are primarily owned by 'native' Taiwanese business people, who under other circumstances might have been tempted to support the Democratic Progressive Party in elections, but who could be deterred by the threat of possible retaliation by the PRC in the event of a DPP electoral victory. And the investments from Taiwan also have the effect of disguising ROC products in PRC-manufactured exports to the USA, so that some appear to come from the PRC, which then becomes the butt of US criticisms over 'unfair' trade surpluses.

The Clinton presidency, the new arguments with Japan over its trade surplus, and official US encouragement for a stronger yen will probably in the short run have the effect of stimulating exports from the NIEs, including Taiwan, as happened in the mid-1980s following the surge in the price of the yen. But unlike in the late 1980s, when the NT dollar appreciated by 40 per cent between 1986 and 1990, i.e. even faster than the yen, in 1994–5 the NT dollar shadowed the US dollar rather than the yen. Between May 1994 and May 1995 it fell 18 per cent against the yen, although it has subsequently recovered somewhat. The resulting difficulties for the Japanese economy will no doubt enhance Taiwan and the PRC more generally as engines of growth for the Asia-Pacific region, especially as they are reinforcing each other's growth. So any deflection of criticism away from Taiwan to the PRC will be of some comfort to the government in Taipei.

Leaving aside these compensations, however, the fundamental problem for the Taiwanese government is that the island is becoming ever more dependent upon the mainland for sustaining its prosperity. Already the mainland is Taiwan's fourth largest trading partner. Even if trade stayed at its current level, the mainland would account for an even greater share of Taiwanese exports after the return of Hong Kong in 1997. Prime Minister Lien Chan has predicted that by the year 2000 the mainland will be Taiwan's largest trading partner, major investing area and main source of trade surplus.[20] The question is how far that dependence upon trade will restrict the government's freedom of manoeuvre. In 1994, 9 per cent of Taiwan's exports were going to the PRC.

Yet there is little that the government can do directly to prevent this growing dependence. It already tries to discourage investors from going to the mainland, but they do so primarily because of economic opportunities there that do not exist on Taiwan. Already in 1990 a survey of a thousand companies showed that 61 per cent, by far the largest proportion, would invest on the mainland because the investment climate on Taiwan was deteriorating.[21] Since trying to crack down on trade or investment with the mainland would have forced it underground, the government's best course is to improve the investment climate on Taiwan, as indeed it is trying to do. But if certain 'sunset' manufacturing industries can no longer survive on Taiwan because of higher costs, company owners will continue to export capital to try to preserve their firms. And if, as seems likely, other Taiwanese companies become attracted by the opportunities offered by the growing market on the mainland, the pressure will continue to mount.

Welfare and income distribution

The demand for state-organized or even state-supported welfare schemes is growing. As noted above, welfare on Taiwan has traditionally been provided by the extended family, rather than the state. The ability of families to continue to bear this burden has, however, been eroded by economic development, demographic changes and increasing geographical as well as social mobility. Demand for state-organized services to relieve the burden on families has been increasing. Between 1986 and 1993 the proportion of the population covered by the three government-organized schemes of labour insurance, farmers' health insurance and the government's own employee insurance rose from 31 per cent to 58 per cent.

The problem is becoming more serious where the elderly are concerned.[22] According to the 1990 census the nuclear family has grown in importance, and the primary type of family unit is now a couple living with their (usually two) children. Some 43.1 per cent of family households come into this category. In addition, almost 11 per cent of households are one-parent families. Increasing numbers of women are employed full-time, leaving them less time to look after dependents.[23]

Yet the proportion of the population aged 65 or over has been steadily increasing. In 1990 it was 6.1 per cent, as compared to 2.5 per cent in 1956. At present only 12 per cent depend upon retirement or annuity pensions for income. Some 60 per cent remain economically active, two-thirds of them working on their own farms. Nevertheless 62 per cent still live with their married children, who provide 61 per cent of their parents' living expenses.

As other pressures on the family increase, so too will the burden of looking after the elderly. Whether families, and especially wives, will continue to accept that they should bear the bulk of the mounting cost of support for dependents in terms of both time and money remains unclear. In a democratizing society there are likely to be mounting pressures for the state to redistribute some of this burden among all citizens through enhanced welfare schemes, which will have an impact on the rest of the economy. For example, one of the goals of the Six-Year Development Programme was the introduction of a universal national health-care system in 1994. Previously health-care had accounted for about 2 per cent of national income. A universal system, however, could not cost less than 4 per cent, and in other developed countries it accounts for around 8 per cent. A universal health-care system on Taiwan might consume resources that are needed, say, for the elderly.

A second area of concern is the increasing income inequality. As was noted above, in the 1980s the disparity between the top and bottom 20 per cent of the population began to grow again, until it reached the same level as at the end of the 1960s.[24] By international standards the gap was not large. Yet in so far as the high degree of equality was often thought to be a factor in Taiwan's economic success, its erosion may be a hindrance. At any rate, the sense of growing inequality has tended to encourage voters to support the DPP rather than the KMT. Certainly the end of the 1980s saw public protests of 'snails without shells', i.e. those, especially young people, who found it impossible to buy or even start buying a flat for themselves because of the enormous increase in land values following the influx of money from export successes.

Labour shortages

Here two problems can be identified. First, Taiwan has effectively enjoyed full employment since the 1960s. More recently, it has been confronted with increasing shortages of unskilled labour. The ratio of vacancies to job-seekers in this category, i.e. those with only primary education, had risen almost fivefold in a decade, from 4.6 in 1983 to 20.8 in 1993. As a result, from the end of the 1980s companies began to employ illegal immigrants. The government responded in 1990 by approving work permits for the first time for limited numbers of guest-workers. By June 1995 the permitted number had risen to 315,919, i.e. 3.5 per cent of the total labour force. Two-thirds of them work in manufacturing.[25]

As a short-term expedient this has helped to alleviate the problem. However, Taiwan is a densely populated island and there are considerable concerns – political, social and cultural – over admitting more immigrants. Thus the labour shortage is likely to continue, constraining business operations and exerting yet another pressure on companies to invest in manufacturing opportunities abroad.

The second problem is less specific but still pervasive. It concerns the work motivation of younger people as the society becomes more prosperous and as the opportunities increase for individual self-fulfilment through means other than work. Just as in Japan, middle-aged and elderly people in Taiwan worry whether the younger generation are prepared to work as hard as people did in the aftermath of Second World War and the civil war against the communists.

Democratization and the role of government

The role of the government in the Taiwanese 'success story' has been a source of considerable contention. Some analysts have argued that Taiwan's success can be attributed to the reluctance of the government to interfere in the workings of the markets. On the one hand there is no doubt that the government has in the past intervened, albeit selectively, to direct economic development along certain paths.[26] On the other hand it is also clear that the government's achievements in this respect have been far from complete. The failure to develop a viable domestic car industry, as mentioned above, is but one example.

Now there is increasing domestic pressure on the government to make way for businesses to run their own affairs and for government to concentrate on setting the parameters for the macroeconomy. Partly this stems from the increasing self-confidence of business people born of years of success. Partly it is the result of the increasing number of scandals incriminating party and government officials in recent years. And partly, too, it is a response to international pressure in the developed world for Taiwan to change its policies before it can be accepted into institutions managing the world economy, such as the World Trade Organization.

The effect of this change of style will be to reduce the government's ability to guide the economy in the directions which it thinks fit. As Taiwan catches up with the technologies of the developed world, it will not be able to save time and effort by learning from the experience of others. The likelihood of wasting resources by developing technologies that ultimately prove fruitless will increase. This will be one more potential obstacle to overcome if the economy is to continue to grow at the same rate as in the past.

The government's manoeuvrability is also threatened by a possible consequence of democratization. It is sometimes argued that competitive party politics has the effect of encouraging parties to bid for voter support by offering material rewards in the form of higher welfare benefits. As has already been seen, there are renewed calls for the government to halt widening inequality, and some signs indicate that both KMT and DPP representatives in the LY have begun to compete over welfare proposals. Indeed, as was emphasized in Chapter 2, if the LY has no incentive to act 'responsibly', individual legislators will indeed compete to offer more attractive welfare proposals, since the publicity involved could help their re-election campaigns. But were that to happen on a significant scale, it would be one further budgetary pressure on the government, which would have to borrow money and thereby withhold resources for business.

The impact of the outside world

The last group of challenges for Taiwanese macroeconomic management can be loosely defined as ones that come from the international environment.

The first is the danger that world trading blocs will develop. At present the danger of the world trading system breaking down into a group of regional blocs may not seem very great, but the government is extremely sensitive to this issue, since its lack of diplomatic recognition would make it very difficult for Taiwan to negotiate market access for its companies. This was one of the main reasons for the government's decision to apply for membership of GATT, now the World Trade Organization (WTO), since, once inside, Taiwan would be able to press for equitable treatment.

The second challenge is the impact of Taiwanese membership of the WTO itself, whenever that is finally agreed. A study by an economic institute in Taipei concluded that over the long term membership of the WTO would add one per cent to Taiwan's economic growth. In the short term, however, there is no doubt that Taiwan would have to make significant concessions to pressures from developed economies. The most obvious of these would affect agriculture, especially rice production. The government has accepted in principle that in the first year after accession to the WTO, rice imports would amount to at least 3 per cent of the domestic market and that by the sixth year this would have risen to 5 per cent, as well as reducing tariffs on imports. The Taiwanese Agricultural Council estimated that this would lead to a fall of 13–15 per cent in domestic rice production over the first six years and that all the concessions would cut farmers' income by US$1 billion annually. Clearly this risks alienating traditional farmer support for the KMT, though the government has promised funds to encourage further diversification.

In addition Taiwan will be forced to remove its ban on imports of cars made in Japan and on Japanese tenders for public construction contracts. Even though Taiwan is proposing to introduce numerical quotas on Japanese cars, there seems no doubt that Taiwan's trade deficit with Japan will grow.

The biggest potential problem, however, of accession to the WTO and

Asia-Pacific Economic Cooperation (APEC) is the impact upon Taiwan's economic relations with the mainland. In principle each side must extend most-favoured-nation status to the other once admitted to the WTO, though this can be excused on the grounds of national security. But Taiwan will find it very difficult to maintain its ban on direct trade with the mainland, even if it is practicable to do so after Hong Kong is returned to the PRC. Either way it is difficult not to believe that trade between the two will grow even more. The Bogor Declaration adopted by the APEC conference in November 1994 commits its signatories to dismantling all policy-based obstacles to trade and investment between them over the next 25 years.

The third challenge is the impact of increased defence spending, which obviously depends on relations with the mainland. Between 1983 and 1994 defence spending fell from 57 to 26 per cent of the national budget, equivalent to a fall from 9.2 to 4.3 per cent of GNP. It may seem curious that this took place at a time when Taiwan was diplomatically more isolated than ever, and in absolute terms defence spending continued to rise, but the economic reforms on the mainland and its opening to the outside world suggested that the danger of invasion was less acute. In more recent years, however, the increasing age of Taiwan's aircraft and naval ships has led it to buy frigates and F-16 and Mirage fighters from the USA and France, not to mention the procurement of its own indigenous fighter. This had already been decided before the PRC held 'test firings' of missiles in the direction of Taiwan in July and August 1995, reawakening a fear of invasion. Now there is talk of Taiwan's buying Patriot anti-missile systems, but these do not come cheap. If the PRC continues to exert military pressure against Taiwan, it seems inevitable that military spending will increase again, thereby reducing government resources available for other needs.

Conclusion

By the early 1990s the internationalization of the Taiwanese economy was far advanced. Its high export/GDP ratio had stabilized. Tariffs had been lowered to a point where, according to the Governor of the Central Bank of China, they effectively amounted to only a little over 4 per cent, and the government had an incentive to keep them low as a way of reducing an otherwise embarrassingly large trade surplus. In the mid-1980s the regime had also introduced measures to strengthen intellectual property rights, and although other governments complained about ineffective enforcement of those rights, the ROC became seriously interested in effective protection as it moved towards a more science-based development path, with its own technological innovations to defend. Between 1986 and 1991 the number of patents approved went up nearly threefold, from 10,526 to 27,281. Half of these were from Chinese and half from foreigners seeking to take advantage of the new circumstances. Since then the rush for foreigners to protect patents has declined, but the number of applications from Chinese has remained roughly constant at around 12,000 per year. And although there were rumblings from peasants about unfair pressure from foreign competition if Taiwan were to join the WTO, the government knew that to regain its membership of international economic organizations it must ensure that it could not be accused by other countries of agricultural or any other kind of protectionism.

Contacts with the outside world were developing rapidly. International telephone traffic grew by roughly 30 per cent annually from the beginning of the 1970s. Foreign travel also increased after the lifting of restrictions at the end of the 1980s, so that people became more internationally-minded. It was estimated that between 1986 and 1991 expenditure on foreign travel by Taiwanese citizens had risen from US\$1.8 billion to \$5.7 billion.[27] By 1992 it was expected that one-fifth of the population would be travelling abroad at some point during the year.

However, the economy was not without its difficulties. Increasing labour shortages meant that some companies had begun to resort to the hire of illegal foreign labour to maintain output. The many surplus workers on the mainland who, unlike Filipinos or Bangladeshis, could speak Mandarin and/or local dialects, were an attractive proposition for local companies, compounding Taiwan's security problems. Once smuggled to Taiwan, they were indistinguishable from local workers and therefore difficult for the police and security services to detect. Perhaps half the fishermen on trawlers operating out of Taiwan had come from the mainland illegally.

There were also uncertainties over the ability of the small and medium-sized companies to cope with the technological upgrading needed to remain ahead of cheaper competitors in Asia and elsewhere, though they always seemed to rise to the challenge. Moreover, an inadequate infrastructure led to increasing problems, as did pollution caused by industrial growth, and the costs involved in cleaning it up. It was possible, too, that as the standard of living rose, people would begin to value increased leisure time and would work less hard. They might also come to demand more state welfare benefits, which would impose extra costs.

All this meant that the high growth rates recorded over the previous 40 years probably could not be sustained. Nevertheless analysts inside and outside the country maintained that an annual growth rate of 6 per cent per year was both desirable and feasible. By coincidence this was the figure suggested by the regime on the mainland as being both desirable and feasible for its own economy in the 1990s, although already in 1991 it had begun to exceed it. But in so far as both the PRC and the ROC were increasingly engaged in economic cooperation, they could help each other to sustain high rates of growth, even if other parts of the world economy were suffering from recession, or (like the USA) were making it more difficult for others to export to them.

In all these respects, then, Taiwan has become a mature, developed, industrial economy, the twelfth largest trading nation in the world. If it were a 'normal' state, it would already be a member of GATT, and membership of the OECD would be under serious discussion, as it has been for South Korea. Yet its anomalous international situation means that these issues still await resolution. Nevertheless Taiwan's economic success has given both its leaders and its people a new self-confidence, which has encouraged them to force the question of its international status back on to international agendas.

Notes

1 *The East Asian Miracle* (OUP for the World Bank, 1993), p. 3.
2 *Asia 1995 Yearbook* (Hong Kong: *Far Eastern Economic Review*, 1995), p. 14.
3 Lee Teng-hui, *Agriculture and Economic Development in Taiwan* (Taichung: Ta-hung, 1983), vol. 3, pp. 1448–9.
4 Several of the subsequent points are taken from *Chung Hua Min Kuo: T'aiwan tich'ü chingchi hsientaihua te lich'eng* [Republic of China: Processes of Economic Modernization in the Taiwan Region] (Taipei: Economic Research Office of the Economic Development Council, 1991), pp. 11–13.
5 Gustav Ranis, 'The Evolution of Policy in a Comparative Perspective: An Introductory Essay', in K.T. Li, *The Evolution of Policy behind Taiwan's Development Success* (New Haven: Yale University Press, 1989), p. 19.
6 For details of government policy towards farming, see Yu-kang Mao, 'Agricultural Development Policies of Taiwan in the Postwar Era', *Industry of Free China*, July 1995, pp. 51–65.
7 Samuel C. Shieh, 'Balance of Payments Adjustment and Financial Internationalization in the ROC', *Industry of Free China*, February 1993, p. 28.

8 *Industry of Free China*, February 1993, p. 53.
9 *T'aiwan tich'ü chingchi hsientaihua te lich'eng*, p. 41; *Industry of Free China*, June 1995, p. 53.
10 *T'aiwan tich'ü chingchi hsientaihua te lich'eng*, p. 88.
11 Paul K.C. Liu, 'Science, Technology and Human Capital Formation', in Gustav Ranis (ed.), *Taiwan: From Developing to Mature Economy* (Boulder: Westview Press, 1992), p. 372.
12 Michael Holday, *Innovation in East Asia: The Challenge to Japan* (Aldershot: Edward Elgar, 1995), pp. 95–135.
13 *T'aiwan tich'ü chingchi hsientaihua te lich'eng*, p. 16.
14 *An Initiative into the Next Century* (Taipei: Coordination and Service Office for Asia-Pacific Regional Operations Center, Council for Economic Planning and Development, 1995), p. 11.
15 Ibid., p. 6.
16 *Far Eastern Economic Review*, 18 March 1993, pp. 44–5.
17 *The Free China Journal*, 26 March 1993, p. 1.
18 *Economic Daily News*, 16 July 1995, p. 5.
19 *Commercial Times*, 19 June 1995 p. 2.
20 *Commercial Times*, May 31 1995, p. 2.
21 Mikio Sumitani et al., *T'aiwan chih chingchi* [Taiwan's Economy] (Taipei: Jenchien Publishing House, 1993), p. 313.
22 Many of the details in the following paragraphs are taken from Paul K.C. Liu, 'Demographic Issues and Trends as reported in the 1990 Census of Taiwan', *Industry of Free China*, August 1993, pp. 41–51.
23 See Lucie Cheng and Ping-chun Hsiung, 'Women, Export-Oriented Growth and the State: The Case of Taiwan', in Joel D. Aberbach et al. (eds), *The Role of the State in Taiwan's Development* (NY and London: M.E. Sharpe, 1994), pp. 321–53.
24 *T'aiwan tich'ü chingchi hsientaihua te lich'eng*, p. 21.
25 *Industry of Free China*, August 1995, pp. 76–7.
26 See R. Wade, *Governing the Market: Economic Theory and the Role of Government in East Asian Industrialization* (Princeton: Princeton University Press, 1990).
27 Shieh, 'Balance of Payments Adjustment', p. 26.

Chapter 4

Pragmatic Diplomacy: Foreign Policy and External Relations

Chiao Chiao Hsieh

Introduction

On 24 August 1992 the Republic of Korea (ROK) extended diplomatic recognition to the People's Republic of China. Consequently Seoul withdrew diplomatic links with the Republic of China on Taiwan and accepted Peking's claim to be China's 'sole legal government'. As Taiwan's last formal diplomatic ally in Asia, the ROK thereby added further difficulties to its diplomatic status. Taiwan was now officially recognized by 29 states, which, except for South Africa and the Vatican, were small countries lacking diplomatic influence. This switch on the ROK's part immediately challenged the validity of the ROC's 'pragmatic diplomacy', which Taipei had actively pursued since July 1988 in its attempts to break out of its diplomatic isolation.

Nevertheless, just 10 days after the loss of the ROK, Taiwan claimed two major diplomatic victories, which were followed by several others. On 2 September, the USA lifted a 10-year ban on arms sales to Taiwan, despite protests from Peking. The repercussions of this policy have led to the opening of new options for Taiwan's military establishment, and to a new beginning for USA–Taiwan relations. Several Western countries, including France (which had signed a contract with Taipei in November to sell 60 Mirage 2000 jet fighters and at least 1,000 short- and medium-range missiles), the Netherlands and Germany, were encouraged to re-evaluate their positions on arms sales to Taiwan, which had been blocked in previous years owing to pressure from Peking.[1] Meanwhile, in December, the USA sent a trade representative to Taiwan for economic talks. This was the first cabinet-level official to go to Taiwan since Washington switched diplomatic recognition from Taipei to Peking in 1979. Furthermore it was reported that the transition paper for President-elect Clinton included a recommendation that the USA should upgrade its official contacts with Taiwan, and the newly elected president was expected to look favourably on the proposal. Taipei welcomed these developments, which suggested that Washington was now putting commerce before China politics in its dealings with Taiwan, and regarded them as clear signals of US interest in strengthening ties with Taiwan. In early 1994 the US Secretary of Transportation, Federico F. Peña, made a rare visit to Taiwan. On his departure he confirmed that the Clinton administration 'is committed to strengthened economic and cultural relations with Taiwan'.

On 8 September 1992 Taiwan and Russia decided to resume government-to-government relations for the first time since 1949, though without official recognition being accorded. Despite warnings from Peking, similar relationships are expected with Ukraine and Belarus, other republics of the former Soviet Union. Further breakthroughs include the increasing flow of cabinet-level visits to Taiwan from Australia, Austria, Belgium, the UK, France, Germany, Italy and many others, visits that would have been almost unthinkable a year or two ago. These developments signify that countries now pay less attention to Peking's diplomatic blockade and that Taipei's 'pragmatic diplomacy', aimed at strengthening or restoring ties with countries that recognize the PRC, has proved of some effect.

This chapter consists of four parts. The first section gives a brief summary of the ROC's diplomatic history from 1949 until 1979, with emphasis on the factors contributing to the ROC's diplomatic development. The second considers the background that gave rise to the current 'pragmatic diplomacy', and the third focuses on its implementation, while the final section assesses its effectiveness.

Diplomatic history, 1949–79

The ROC's Cold War diplomacy from 1949 to 1979 can be broadly divided into two periods. During the first period, from 1949 to 1970, the ROC depended almost totally on the USA for security protection and national development, even counting on it to carry out the task of national reunification. During this period Taipei adopted three foreign policy strategies: the so-called 'military counterattack', 'political counterattack' and 'foreign aid'. Its most important foreign policy objectives were to secure its relations with the USA, to protect its seat at the UN and to maintain its existing level of diplomatic recognition. Decision-makers in Taipei believed that as long as it stayed loyal to the US and formed a close anti-communist alliance with it, its chance of returning to the mainland and winning the diplomatic war with the PRC could be maximized. The ROC's efforts did succeed in isolating the PRC internationally and prevented it from joining the UN. Meanwhile the ROC was recognized, though only by Western countries, as the sole legal government of China. It was one of the 'Big Five' at the UN Security Council.

Three factors contributed to Taiwan's favourable position. First, the USA's positive support was a significant force in keeping a large number of Western countries on the ROC's side. The Korean war had recommitted the USA to actively supporting the ROC'S anti-communist cause. Since the USA was the unchallenged leader of the free world, its China policy had a profound impact on the foreign policies of many non-communist countries, especially in Western Europe and Latin America. Secondly, the PRC's hardline policy of world communism provoked general international antagonism. During this period the PRC mobilized both domestic and international forces to conduct anti-Western movements and to promote revolutionary war against 'revolutionary regimes' in Asia, Africa, Latin America and the Middle East. These actions won it little international sympathy. Its international image and reputation sank to its lowest point during the Cultural Revolution (1966–76). Thirdly, there were the ROC's aid programmes to less developed countries in Africa and Latin America, whose support was important for the ROC's membership of the UN.

The second period, from the ROC's withdrawal from the UN in 1971 to US recognition of the PRC in 1979, was a critical turning point in the ROC's Cold War diplomacy. During this period Taipei suffered a series of setbacks, including Peking's admission to the UN in 1971, the signing of the joint US-PRC communiqué in Shanghai in 1972, Japan's recognition of the PRC in the same year, and the US derecognition of the ROC in 1979. In effect, even before the ROC's UN débâcle, international support for Taipei had shown signs of weakening. In 1970, for example, Canada extended recognition to the PRC by accepting Peking's claim to Taiwan without explicitly endorsing it. The Canadian action had a tremendous negative impact on Taiwan as it was the first non-communist country to recognize the PRC since France in 1964. Soon afterwards a domino derecognition effect took place. By 1979 only 21 countries maintained diplomatic links with Taipei, whereas 117 had official relations with Peking. In all, from January 1971 to January 1979, 46 countries changed allegiance in their China policies. Similarly, most of the international governmental organizations (IGOs) related to the UN, including UNESCO, the World Health Organization (WHO) and the Food and Agriculture Organization (FAO), expelled Taipei and seated Peking. Towards the end of 1979 the ROC maintained membership in only four UN specialized agencies: the International Monetary Fund (IMF), the International Bank for Reconstruction and Development (IBRD), the International Finance Committee (IFC), and the International Development Association (IDA) – all were later lost to Taiwan in the 1980s – and in nine other IGOs and 257 international non-governmental organizations (INGOs), mostly non-political.

Three interrelated factors explain the ROC's diplomatic misfortunes. First, from 1979 the PRC had itself adopted a pragmatic approach to its foreign policy, which was designed to improve its international image and to facilitate its modernization programmes. Its aim was to promote a peaceful environment within China itself and in its relations with the outside world. This new approach effectively removed the diplomatic wall between the PRC and the non-communist countries at the expense of Taiwan. Secondly, the USA decided to normalize relations with the PRC, and its waning support for the ROC, expressed clearly by President Nixon's visit to China in 1972, influenced the China policies of many countries. Thirdly, the ROC continued to practise dogmatically the policy of 'no coexistence with the (Chinese) communists'. Although most countries, in recognizing the PRC, usually accepted Peking's claim to be the only legitimate ruler of China, they did not have to suspend all their ties with Taipei. In most cases, it was Taipei's inflexibility that led to a breakdown of relations. The same applied to its relations with most international organizations. For example, in 1971 a motion in the UN had been put forward to retain the ROC's membership in the General Assembly, thus obtaining 'dual representation', but Taipei decided to pre-empt the motion and walk out. Such an uncompromising and emotional 'one China' policy left other countries with little choice but to make a complete switch to the PRC.

The defeat at the UN and the USA's new China policy had a critical effect on the ROC's international status and future diplomacy. Taiwan was forced to adopt a more flexible and realistic approach to its foreign policy – the 'substantive diplomacy', which emphasized the ROC's external economic and trade contacts. Although at the beginning of the 1980s this new diplomacy demonstrated more accommodation and less dogmatism, its earlier identity crisis and isolation had caused irreparable damage.

The move to 'pragmatic diplomacy'

Many countries which, in the 1970s, regarded Taiwan as having few options other than to seek accommodation with Peking have, since the 1980s, changed their opinion. They have become aware of Taiwan's 'economic miracle', perceived technological strength, and its more flexible attitudes to diplomacy. Many of them, while still maintaining diplomatic relations with the PRC, have established trade offices or similar institutions in Taiwan and likewise have allowed Taipei to open offices in their respective capitals to do 'official things unofficially'. Meanwhile a large number of Third World countries began to look to Taiwan's economic success as a model for their own development. They also took advantage of Taiwan's overseas aid programmes.

In 1983 such developments began to worry Peking, which feared that they might give Taiwan more international legitimacy and hence make its leaders less willing to negotiate about reunification. Indeed after decades of separation and hostility Taiwan had become even more 'indigestible' to the PRC, as existing political, economic, social and psychological differences between the two systems grew ever wider. From 1949 to 1978 the PRC's reunification policy was based primarily upon military invasion. After 1979 this hardline position softened in order to promote a peaceful image and to encourage modernization programmes. In 1984 the PRC proposed peaceful reunification on the basis of 'one country, two systems'. According to this formula, Taiwan would have been able to maintain a high degree of autonomy as a special administrative region *under* Peking. It would have been allowed to keep its own armed forces, to preserve its current socio-economic system, and to continue its economic and cultural links with other countries, and Peking would have agreed not to interfere in its 'local affairs'. However, Peking would not drop its insistence on sovereignty over Taiwan. Nor would it renounce the use of force to bring about reunification, should peaceful means fail. These positions were reiterated at the Fourteenth National Party Congress of the PRC in October 1992, at which new policies were added, including 'No recognition of Taiwan as an equal political entity', and 'Firm opposition to Taiwan's flexible diplomacy'.

External influences

Towards the end of the 1980s and the beginning of the 1990s, international power relationships began to be transformed. The end of the Cold War, marked by the decline of international communism and the break-up of the Soviet Union, has brought forth a new international order. This new reality allows for a degree of integration and mutual interdependence, encouraging countries to adopt a more flexible and less dogmatic approach when conducting their foreign affairs. This transition to a 'new order' is a dynamic process and still under way.

The new world order has helped Taipei in the conduct of its diplomacy, allowing it to promote external relations in a multipolar world, not simply by formal diplomacy, but by using its economic strength and political and social progress as diplomatic tools to win friends and influence. Taiwan's gains in this new set of power relationships are clearly described in the following observation:

> The most conspicuous beneficiary has been Taiwan, whose political non-existence in the eyes of its trading partners for more than a decade has been at odds with its status as the world's 13th-largest trading nation. The most prominent loser appears to be Peking, which can no longer command deference from the world community, even in areas where it has direct interests ... This is the basic dismantling of the Cold War architecture ... It is a natural levelling out of the effects of the Cold War when Peking's importance was heightened by tensions with Moscow and Taipei's position was ignored. Now each country in the region [of Asia] and those outside are trying to find their natural place in the new power equation, which is based more on economic than on political factors.[2]

Indeed to some extent the end of the Cold War has reduced the PRC's leverage in world affairs and increased Taiwan's. Taiwan's strengthening position can also be explained by the simple fact that the PRC has become one of the few remaining communist countries. The departure of hardliners in such countries leaves the PRC fewer opportunities to influence their China policies. Eastern Europe as it is now and the new former Soviet republics have offered Taipei a new diplomatic battleground on which to challenge Peking. In this regard Taipei has some advantages over Peking in terms of its economic power and its intermediate-level technology. Most of the former communist countries are seeking to transform their faltering economic systems into market-oriented ones, and thus provide trade openings for Taiwan.

The Tiananmen incident in June 1989 also had an impact on the ROC's foreign relations. It influenced a shift in international opinion against the PRC. Severe international criticism made Peking a temporary pariah, and differences over human rights, prison labour and trade policy, which were muted before 1989, have since dominated the PRC's bilateral relations with the USA. The ending of strategic collaboration has further hardened the US attitude, which has now become less tolerant and conciliatory. Meanwhile Taiwan exploited the situation to its advantage. It was at this time that the ROC's democratization process began to show results, so that Taipei could project itself as a 'better China'. It moved quickly to establish formal diplomatic ties with Grenada and to open an official trade mission to Vanuatu. The Tiananmen incident has also acted as a brake on the 'mainland fever' which was sweeping Taiwan and has diluted whatever hopes the people of Taiwan might have had about the PRC's peaceful offensive for reunification.

Internal factors: demands for change

By the mid-1980s decision-makers on Taiwan were convinced that, in order to secure the ROC's long-term survival, it was imperative to launch revolutionary policy adjustments both at home and in foreign affairs. These included, internally, political democratization, and externally, a less rigid mainland policy and a more flexible, pragmatic foreign policy. It was hoped that 'reforms may help improve our international image and our relations with the West'.[3]

In 1986 the KMT government began the series of political reforms outlined in Chapter 2. The aim of the reforms is in short to 'Taiwanize' the island's politics, a process that is still under way. A consequence has been to put relations with the mainland back on the political agenda, because of the DPP's demand for independence, or at least a public referendum on the issue. It insists that Taiwan is a sovereign independent entity. The DPP's foreign policy platform holds that 'Taiwan is Taiwan, and China is China. Taiwan should develop its own international relations, including membership in the UN and all other international organizations on the basis of independent sovereignty and under the name of "Taiwan".'[4]

The year 1987 marked a major turning point in Taiwan's relations with mainland China: the KMT government lifted the 38-year-old martial law and allowed its residents to visit mainland relatives for the first time since 1949. Since then Taipei has worked to promote peaceful coexistence and competition instead of the previous military confrontation with Peking. In 1988 direct trade via Hong Kong was legalized. Indirect Taiwanese investment across the Straits was also tacitly approved. In June 1989, at the KMT's Thirteenth National Congress,

President Lee declared that his government's current policy was to give priority to the development and security of Taiwan. He further admitted that there was no way in which the KMT government could exercise its rule on the mainland for the time being and that it would be better to be courageous enough to admit this fact and map out practical and pragmatic policies based on effective rule within its own area of control. Since then the direction of Taiwan's new mainland policy has been to promote reunification under Lee's terms of 'one country, two governments'. In May 1990 Lee repeated this proposal, with modifications, in his inaugural speech: 'The KMT government is willing to hold talks with the PRC within the one-China framework and on a government-to-government basis *with equal status*.' This 'one country, two equal governments' framework differs from the PRC's 'one country, two systems' proposal, which requires Taiwan's recognition of Peking's ultimate sovereignty. It has since become the basis of the ROC's mainland policy.

In May 1991 the KMT government terminated the 42-year-old civil war with Peking. The ROC now formally acknowledged the existence of two equal political entities in two separate areas of one country. It has given up the intention of using force to retake the mainland. Thus it has become clear that Taipei wants an environment in which Taipei and Peking can compete and coexist peacefully. The reunification policy, however, remains principally and theoretically unchanged. In March 1992 Taiwan's premier Hau Pei-ts'un reiterated this 'one China, but not now' position: 'Abandoning mainland sovereignty would cost us our "basic position" ... the division between Taiwan and the mainland will remain for some time even though mutual exchanges have substantially increased.'[5]

Until 1995 relationships between Taiwan and the mainland improved considerably. One example was the Singaporean talks in April 1994. In order to solve some 'practical problems', such as trade and investment protection, the hijacking of passenger airliners from the PRC to Taiwan, possible direct air links, etc., higher-level contacts between the intermediary organizations of the two sides – Taiwan's Straits Exchange Foundation (SEF) and the PRC's Association for Relations Across the Taiwan Straits (ARATS) – took place in Singapore. Meanwhile the volume of informal contacts on the socio-economic level increased greatly.

On 30 January 1995 President Jiang Zemin made a speech on bilateral relations, adopting a conciliatory tone towards Taiwan. The speech made eight points:

(1) the one-China principle was fundamental and should serve as the premise for peaceful reunification;

(2) Peking had no objection to Taiwan's developing non-governmental economic and cultural ties;

(3) the PRC had consistently proposed negotiations for peaceful reunification; and,

(4) both sides should strive to achieve it. By implication, if negotiations went smoothly, Taiwan might be able to retain its own government in a reunited China.

(5) cross-Straits economic ties should be developed for the prosperity of both sides;

(6) the 5,000-year-old civilization was a bond linking all Chinese together;

(7) all inhabitants of Taiwan were Chinese compatriots;

(8) official Taiwanese leaders were welcome to visit the mainland, and Peking's leaders were willing to visit Taiwan if they received an official invitation.

President Lee took great personal interest in this speech and responded with his own six points:

(1) unification should be sought on the basis of recognition of the reality of the current division;

(2) cultural exchanges should be used to strengthen cross-Straits contacts;

(3) it was necessary to increase economic and other mutually beneficial exchanges;

(4) both sides should be allowed parallel representation in international bodies, where leaders could meet on the basis of equality;

(5) both sides should hold to the principle of the peaceful resolution of all disputes;

(6) both sides should collaborate to maintain the prosperity of Hong Kong and Macao.

Although a great deal of negotiation was still needed before any agreement could be achieved, the tone of these exchanges was extremely conciliatory. All this changed, however, with President Lee's 'private' visit to the USA in June 1995, which broke assurances that US administrations had given to Peking right up to the last minute that this would not be allowed. The PRC responded furiously, cancelling a regular meeting between ARATS and the SEF, attacking President Lee personally and vituperatively, and then in July and August organizing 'trials' for missiles close to the Taiwanese coast, which required diversion of shipping. This was reminiscent of the war of words across the Taiwan Straits in the 1950s, and set back any improvement in relations at least until after the Taiwanese presidential elections in March 1996.

Lee's 'pragmatic diplomacy'

The 'pragmatic diplomacy' developed principally in line with the new mainland policy. While the latter can be summarized as 'one country, two equal governments' and envisages long-term coexistence of the two governments, the former suggests a 'tolerance', or even subtle encouragement, of international dual recognition.

'Pragmatic diplomacy' is also known as 'elastic', 'economic' or 'flexible' diplomacy. Peking, however, is more dismissive, calling it 'dollar', 'chequebook' or 'silver-bullet' diplomacy. In July 1988 Lee gave the first official pronouncement of this strategy: 'The ROC will adopt a more pragmatic, flexible and forward-looking approach to develop a foreign policy based primarily on substantive relations.'[6] This diplomatic pragmatism was demonstrated in March 1989, when Lee paid a four-day state visit to Singapore, which recognized neither the ROC nor the PRC at the time, but maintained close contacts with both. On his return he commented: 'When a country wishes to have diplomatic relations with Peking, it does not necessarily mean that the ROC has to sever its contact with that country. Peking's diplomatic gains, in other words, need not be interpreted as the ROC's total loss as it has been.'[7]

Later, in April, Lien Chan, then Taiwan's Foreign Minister, put this new strategy more succinctly: 'The ROC will insist upon its policy of national reunification under freedom, democracy and an equitable distribution of wealth, but will exercise a certain flexibility and pragmatism in its diplomatic manoeuvring to meet the demands of reality.'[8] According to Lee, the purpose of this new diplomacy was to protect the ROC's interests and rights and to enable it to assume its proper role in international affairs and activities.[9] As he declared in June 1989:

> The ultimate goal of the foreign policy of the ROC is to safeguard the integrity of the nation's sovereignty. We should have the courage to face the reality that we are unable for the time being to exercise effective jurisdiction on the mainland. Only in that way

will we not inflate ourselves and entrap ourselves, and be able to come up with pragmatic plans appropriate to the changing times and environment.

The declared objectives of Taipei's new diplomacy are:

(1) to consolidate and strengthen existing diplomatic ties through cooperation in the fields of finance, economy, transportation, industry, fisheries, agriculture, medical care;
(2) to develop and upgrade substantive ties with countries without diplomatic relations with Taiwan through bilateral cooperation in such areas as trade, culture, technology, environmental protection, and to establish semi-official relations; and
(3) to participate or resume participation in international organizations and activities according to a more flexible formula.[10] In short, while the government's political reform aims to 'Taiwanize' politics, in foreign policy it wants to 'internationalize' the island. The latter includes building Taiwan into an international finance and banking centre, and developing communication links around the world, as described in Chapter 3.

The implementation of 'pragmatic diplomacy'

(1) Countries recognizing the ROC
Of the 31 countries with which the ROC currently has diplomatic ties, ten are in Africa, one in Europe (Vatican City), sixteen in Latin America, and four in the South Pacific. It has no diplomatic connections at all with countries in North America, the Middle East and Asia.

Relations with South Africa and some African states   In 1988 Taipei maintained three diplomatic relationships in Africa, with South Africa, Malawi and Swaziland. Since 1989 five African countries have resumed diplomatic relations with Taiwan: Liberia in 1989, Lesotho and Guinea-Bissau in 1990, the Central African Republic in 1991 and Niger in 1992. Liberia had established ties in 1959 and suspended them in 1979. Lesotho established them in 1966 and suspended them in 1983. The Central African Republic established them in 1962, suspended them in 1964, renewed them in 1968 and suspended them again in 1976. Niger established them in 1963 and suspended them in 1974. The first three broke relations with Peking in order to establish ties with Taipei.

Liberia's decision to resume ties with Taipei was significant, because it was the first time a country that had cut ties with the ROC to befriend the PRC had reversed the decision. In December 1993 the new Liberian government, led by the Basotho Congress Party, re-established diplomatic ties with Peking. Taipei, however, chose to remain silent on the matter. It has not withdrawn its diplomatic personnel, nor terminated its assistance programmes. Apparently it hopes to explore the possibility of a two-China policy, as it may do in Lesotho, which terminated ties with Taipei in January 1994 in similar circumstances. However, Taipei still maintains eight diplomatic posts on the African continent, while Burkina Faso (previously Upper Volta) re-established ties with Taiwan in February 1994, after the latter promised substantial amounts of economic, medical, industrial and commercial aid. In January 1996 Senegal re-established diplomatic relations with Taiwan, after previously recognizing it between 1960 and 1964, and 1969 and 1971.

The Central African Republic broke ties with Peking after relations were established with Taipei. The case of Niger was more dramatic. The PRC had put pressure on Niger to withdraw its diplomatic approach to the ROC. After a six-week saga during which Niger changed its mind three times, the diplomatic zigzag between Taipei and Peking was finally straightened out. Peking suspended diplomatic links and all bilateral agreements with Niger, including the withdrawal of a group of doctors it had dispatched as part of an aid package. For Niger the stakes were a hard US$50 million in aid from Taiwan versus vague offers from the PRC of an interest-free loan. Taipei claimed that these diplomatic gains were the result of 'pragmatic diplomacy', in which aid was used to win friends. In fact, they were also partly due to the waning influence of the PRC throughout the continent of Africa. Currently the PRC has diplomatic ties with 45 African states. Its aid programmes concentrate on Egypt, Kenya, Nigeria, Zaire and Zambia, though it was said in November 1992 that Taiwan had established some sort of rapport with Zambia, previously one of Peking's strongest supporters in Africa.

Of all these countries South Africa matters the most to the ROC diplomatically, politically and economically. Because of its policy of apartheid, South Africa long suffered from international isolation and hostility. Since the 1960s the common fate of isolation and an anti-communist ideology drew Taipei and Pretoria together. But at first they were hesitant to formalize their relationship: Taiwan feared such recognition might cost it support from the black-majority African states, essential to its diplomatic battle at the UN, while Pretoria's China policy was said to be not so much pro-Taipei as anti-Peking. After 1971 such considerations evaporated as Taiwan's relations with black African states deteriorated, and as a result of the PRC's new foreign policy initiative. In 1976, out of mutual sympathy, political necessity and economic interests, the ROC and South Africa raised their consular relations to formal diplomatic status. In 1985 Chinese were elevated to the status of 'honorary whites'. Today the ROC is South Africa's sixth largest trading partner, while South Africa is the ROC's biggest trading partner in Africa. There are more than 120 Taiwan-owned factories in South Africa, which is a major market for Taiwan's consumer goods and in turn supplies Taiwan with uranium and coal. It is reported that the two have shared military intelligence and conducted joint nuclear research.

Since the departure of the ROC from the UN, South Africa has become even more important diplomatically to Taipei. At present relations between the two still seem cordial. Nevertheless clouds loom. For years Peking was a critic of South Africa's white government, but after 1991 it took a softer line and hinted that it might be ready to contemplate diplomatic ties, providing Pretoria gave up apartheid and withdrew recognition of the ROC. Given that the first condition has been fulfilled, it is highly likely that South Africa will be Peking's next diplomatic target. In October 1992 Nelson Mandela, then leader of the African National Congress, paid a visit to the PRC, which greatly troubled Taipei. Pretoria and Peking have now exchanged unofficial representative offices, which was a first step towards full recognition in the cases of Israel and the ROK. Two-way trade and bilateral cooperation are also on the increase. So far, however, the ANC government has refrained from recognizing the PRC, despite the latter's assistance during the years of struggle. Its leaders have contemplated attempting dual recognition of the two Chinas, but the likelihood of South Africa's switching sides at some future time is nevertheless increasing. Were that to happen, it is theoretically possible that countries such as Lesotho, Swaziland and Malawi would follow suit, since they maintain close relations with South Africa.

Relations with Latin America   Among the 33 Latin American countries, the ROC at present maintains diplomatic ties with 16: seven in Central America (Belize, Costa Rica, El Salvador, Guatemala, Honduras, Nicaragua and Panama), eight in the Caribbean (the Bahamas, the Dominican Republic, Dominica, Grenada, Haiti, St Christopher, St Lucia and St Vincent) and one in South America (Paraguay). Relations with Belize, the Bahamas and Grenada were established in 1990; relations with

Nicaragua were resumed after a five-year suspension. Again these diplomatic successes were largely results of Taipei's flexible diplomacy. Uruguay's recognition of the PRC in 1989 was the ROC's only major diplomatic setback in Latin America during the 1980s.

During the period 1960 to 1985 the ROC dispatched 46 assistance missions and carried out projects in 23 Latin American countries. These assistance programmes originally concentrated on agricultural cultivation, and then moved towards industrial and technical cooperation. Since mid-1984 the ROC has launched a 'Caribbean Basin Initiative' to provide more technical assistance and to promote Taiwanese investments in the Caribbean and Central America. In July 1990 it established an International Economic Cooperation Fund to help improve the economies of some Latin American countries. Today more and more of these countries, including some which have no diplomatic ties with the ROC, welcome Taipei's technical assistance, capital investment and trade. Currently nine countries – Argentina, Bolivia, Brazil, Chile, Colombia, Ecuador, Mexico, Peru and Venezuela – maintain official relations with Peking and have allowed Taipei to establish representative offices in their capitals. Five of them – Argentina, Bolivia, Brazil, Chile and Mexico – have opened offices in Taipei. These non-political offices, in practice, are 'underground' embassies.

Another device of Taipei's 'pragmatic diplomacy' has been 'visit diplomacy'. Regardless of diplomatic ties, Taipei invites foreign dignitaries with the purpose of influencing their perception of Taiwan. This device has been widely used in promoting Taiwan's relations with Latin American countries, as well as the USA. Between July 1990 and June 1991 about 330 Latin American dignitaries visited Taiwan, including the President of Costa Rica, the Vice-President of Panama, the Vice-President of the Dominican Republic, and prime ministers from St Vincent and Grenada.

Relations with the Vatican The Vatican is the only European state still recognizing the ROC.[11] For years, however, the relationship has not seemed entirely stable. In order to reacquire the right of the Roman Catholic Church to operate openly on the mainland, the Vatican has reportedly made overtures to the PRC and may sacrifice its relations with Taipei. But this has not yet occurred because the PRC demands that the Vatican promise non-interference in Peking's religious affairs, as well as terminating its ties with Taipei. The Tiananmen massacre of 1989 may also have temporarily delayed the Vatican's shift.

Taipei values its ties with the Vatican. It regards the connection as a diplomatic asset when dealing with other European countries, and a help in sustaining diplomatic links with Catholic states in Central and South America. If the PRC succeeds in persuading the Vatican to cut ties with the ROC, then these countries might follow suit, especially if Peking offers them attractive inducements in terms of aid or trade. This would be a serious diplomatic loss for Taipei.

Relations with South Pacific nations   ROC–PRC diplomatic rivalry has also reached into the South Pacific where, among the 15 island states, Taipei has been recognized by Tonga, Naura, Tuvalu, the Solomon Islands and Papua New Guinea since 1972, 1975, 1979, 1983 and 1995 respectively. These relations, which are sealed by Taipei's aid pro- grammes, including cash grants, development assistance and technical expertise, remain generally stable. For example, Taipei has helped Tonga in airport construction and agricultural and fishery development. In 1989 it also funded the construction of a stadium for the South Pacific Mini Games held there. Similarly Taipei has funded a hospital construction project in Honiara, capital of the Solomon Islands. It has also been involved in several other economic development projects. It is said that Taiwan has interests in the marine resources of the Solomon Islands, but such economic motivations should be taken as secondary to Taipei's aim of maintaining a diplomatic presence.

Following the Tiananmen massacre, Taipei intensified efforts to strengthen relations with other Pacific island states, including those that maintained diplomatic ties with the PRC. These efforts have included opening ROC trade missions in Papua New Guinea and in Vanuatu, similar to the ROC Trade Mission in Fiji. In March 1988, much to the dismay of the PRC, Taiwan's official representative body in Suva, the East Asia Trade Centre, was upgraded and renamed the ROC Trade Mission, with consular privileges and immunities. The PRC protested to the Fiji government, but the latter seemed determined to pursue a semi- official relationship with Taiwan. Apparently Taipei offered Fiji the quid pro quo of financial assistance.

(2) Non-official relations
Relations with the USA   The US decision in September 1992 to sell 150 F-16 fighters to Taiwan marked an important victory for Taiwan and a defeat for the PRC on an issue which both governments have been manoeuvring around since the early 1980s. It gave a boost to Taiwan's

morale, which was badly needed after the ROK's diplomatic switch to the PRC in August 1992.

A watershed in US–ROC postwar relations occurred in 1979, with Washington's recognition of the PRC at Taiwan's expense, since when relations between the two have been unofficial, guided principally by four documents: the 1972 Shanghai Communiqué, the 1979 Joint Communiqué on the Establishment of Diplomatic Relations between the USA and the PRC, the 1979 Taiwan Relations Act (TRA), and in 1982 the Second Shanghai Communiqué on Arms Sales to Taiwan. The relationship with the USA continues to be an important factor influencing Taipei's diplomacy and status.

Briefly, the documents hold that the USA recognizes the government of the PRC as the sole legal government of China; that there is but one China and Taiwan is part of it; that the USA will continue to preserve and promote extensive, close and friendly commercial, cultural and other relations with Taiwan without official government representation and without formal diplomatic relations; that the Taiwan issue should be settled in a peaceful manner only by the Chinese themselves; and that the USA will continue to provide Taiwan with arms of a defensive character, which should be gradually reduced, either in qualitative or in quantitative terms, over an unspecified period of time.

Under the TRA Taiwan was to be treated as an entity on a par with 'foreign countries, nations, states, governments, or similar entities' as far as US law was concerned. Furthermore Taiwan would be able to benefit from 'programmes, transactions and other relations' of the USA, especially with regard to the right to litigation in US courts, immigration quotas, nuclear exports, private investment, and protection and membership of international organizations. Thus the TRA provided a legal framework for continued relations between Taiwan and the USA. As far as Washington was concerned, the ROC government no longer existed but was now 'Taiwan'.

The evolution of post-1979 US–Taiwan relations can be divided into three phases. The first phase, from 1979 to the second Communiqué in 1982, was the period of adjustment; the second, from 1982 until President Bush's F-16 decision in September 1992, saw a more settled and stable relationship between the two; and the third, beginning with the arms purchase in 1992, saw a steady strengthening of ties between Washington and Taipei.

In the first phase, both Taiwan and the USA worked to find a way to build their new relationship. At the time of derecognition, the United

States terminated some of the 59 treaties and agreements existing between the two countries, while others lapsed or were amended. The termination of the 1954 Mutual Defence Treaty was the most damaging as far as the ROC's security and military interests were concerned.

In the second phase the relationship between the USA and Taiwan was stabilized, to include semi-official political interactions based on the TRA and economic, social and cultural exchanges. Among these activities economic ties appeared to be the most complicated and troublesome.

At the political level, a notionally non-governmental American Institute in Taiwan (AIT) is now based in Taipei and Kaohsiung, and its counterpart, the Taipei Economic and Cultural Representative Office (formerly the Coordinating Council for North American Affairs, or CCNAA) has its main office in Washington, DC, and branches in eleven US cities – New York, Chicago, Houston, Atlantic City, Seattle, San Francisco, Los Angeles, Honolulu, Boston, Miami and Kansas City. These are the functional equivalents of embassies and consulates-general.

Economically the USA has for years been Taiwan's largest trading partner, with a persistent and huge trade imbalance in favour of Taiwan. Since 1984, the USA has put pressure on Taiwan to remedy this situation. Taiwan has responded with measures that include sending 'Buy American' missions, easing import restrictions and reducing import duties. It has also negotiated solutions to disputes over intellectual property rights, insurance, agriculture, fishery, taxes and telecommunications. Since 1987, owing to the rapid rise of protectionist sentiment in the USA, Taiwan has taken steps to reduce its trade dependence on the USA and has acquired new trading partners.

Socially and culturally, Taipei has relied heavily on 'visit diplomacy'. Since the US government followed a very strict interpretation of unofficiality (contacts between ROC representatives and US officials had to take place outside official executive premises), the CCNAA invited Americans who were not currently federal government officials, but who might have a say in policy-making (not necessarily in the foreign policy area) to visit Taiwan. The number of these visitors usually exceeds a thousand a year. Among them, approximately 13 per cent are members of Congress (and their family members), 12 per cent are Congressional legislative assistants, 43 per cent state and local officials, 10 per cent ex-government or party officials, 16 per cent important members of civic organizations, and 5 per cent academics.[12] The purpose of such visits is to build up an 'unofficial bridge' to gain access to policy-makers. Taipei has conducted this strategy with great subtlety, and it has proved satisfactory. As Governor of Arkansas, Bill Clinton visited Taiwan four times and is said to have a 'rather good' impression of the island.

Meanwhile there has been a steady increase of people-to-people contacts, including tourism and academic, sports and cultural exchanges. Taipei hopes these 'lower-level' contacts will foster mutual understanding and cement friendships between countries. Currently a total of 103 agreements have been signed in such areas as education, customs duties, postal administration, air transport and technological cooperation.

In the third phase the F-16 sale appears to have opened a new chapter in the development of US-Taiwan relations. Taipei seemed to feel more comfortable with the Clinton administration, especially after Washington despatched Trade Representative Carla Hills to Taiwan for an official visit, apparently anticipating Peking's possibly adverse reaction by arranging a parallel visit to Peking by US Commerce Secretary Barbara Franklin. Although the trip was ostensibly to pressurize Taiwan into opening its markets, Mrs Hills's meetings with President Lee and Foreign Minister Frederick Chien were hailed by both sides as 'a historic beginning, an ice-breaking move'.[13]

Taipei expects that more formal links will follow. This hope is based not only on the new US arms-sale policy, and Washington's open support for Taiwan's membership of GATT/WTO, but also on the possible deterioration of US–PRC relations. It is likely, however, that US relations with the PRC will remain essentially unchanged. The USA will continue to respect the 'one China' policy adopted thirteen years ago by President Jimmy Carter while moving economically and politically closer to Taiwan. The reasoning is simple: Taiwan's 20 million people may be richer and 'freer', but the PRC has 1.2 billion people and the political power and military strength to influence world affairs; important issues, such as the Korean conflict, the Cambodian question and arms limitation talks, cannot be effectively resolved without Peking's participation and cooperation.

Thus the ROC is left with little chance of improving official political ties with the USA and a change in US government or public opinion is highly unlikely. The F-16 decision, which Taiwan hailed as a 'major breakthrough' and hoped to use as a stepping-stone to improve ties with the USA and other states, should be taken as a unique case. According to President Bush, the decision 'does not change the commitment of this administration and its predecessors' to the US–PRC 1982 Shanghai

Communiqué.[14] Rather the sale, worth as much as US$5.8 billion, was said to be motivated predominantly by election-year politics to save defence-related jobs, as well as being a response to Peking's recent purchase of Russian SU-27 planes. From the US perspective, Peking's move to acquire modern military technology has changed the military balance along the Taiwan Straits and hence justified the US resumption of arms sales to Taiwan.

In the future the USA may further modify its policy towards Taiwan, for either economic or strategic reasons. It may even consider upgrading its official contacts with Taiwan, as was recommended to the Clinton administration. But the possibility that the USA might resume diplomatic ties with 'the ROC' or recognize a 'Republic of Taiwan' seems unrealistic, even though the Speaker in the US House of Representatives, Newt Gingrich, has called for that.

Relations with Japan   Japan is an exceptional case in ROC diplomacy. Japan's postwar foreign policy was predominantly concerned with economics, and thus its principal policy towards the two Chinese entities has always been to develop the most profitable relations possible with each. Accordingly, Japan has conducted a very peculiar 'one China' policy in principle, but a 'two Chinas' policy in practice. Until September 1972 Japan's diplomatic and other official relations were exclusively with the ROC, but it traded with both Chinas. In September 1972, when relations with the PRC were normalized, Japan reversed this policy.

Until then Taipei was tolerant of Japan's two-pronged China policy and its practice of separating politics and economics because it needed Japanese diplomatic and political support. There was also a strong economic interest. After 1972 the ROC and Japan handled their relations through Taiwan's Association of East Asian Relations (AEAR) in Tokyo and Japan's Taipei Interchange Association in Taipei. In May 1992, after a prolonged effort by Taipei, the AEAR was renamed the Taiwan Economic and Cultural Office, which in a sense has upgraded its status.

At present Japan is Taiwan's second most important trade partner. Bilateral trade grew steadily during the 1980s, but always in favour of Japan, and this trend has increased. In recent years Japan has also stepped up technological cooperation with Taiwan. In 1991 two-way trade reached a record US$24.3 billion. It is understandable, therefore, that relations between the two are easily strained by trade issues. Taipei has taken measures to reduce this chronic imbalance, promoting slogans such as 'Purchase only from areas other than Japan' and 'Boycott Japanese goods', and has urged Japan to increase purchases from Taiwan. The situation, however, has hardly changed.

Fundamental to the insoluble trade problem has been Japan's uncompromising attitude. Japan is aware that Taiwan needs its support and friendship more than it needs Taiwan's. However, the Japanese government mostly takes the PRC's political and economic interests more seriously than Taiwan's, and it could be said to have deliberately ignored Taiwan's interests.

In May 1990 President Lee criticized Japan's attitude to Taiwan in a newspaper interview:

> In the eyes of the Japanese government the ROC does not exist. In all its bilateral dealings with Taiwan, be it diplomatic, trade, cultural or technological, the Japanese government has deliberately avoided any direct official contact or negotiation with Taiwan, leaving Taipei with no choice but to accept a fait accompli.[15]

The Japanese government defended its position by saying that Japan and Taiwan have no diplomatic relations, hence no basis or proper channel for direct communication.[16] Indeed the lack of official ties has put Taipei in a difficult and weak position. But as Lee further pointed out: 'Without diplomatic ties, communication is still possible. Taiwan's relations with the ASEAN nations, the US, some European states, are cases in point.'[17] Here again politics intrude – there is no way in which Japan could develop or promote its relations with Taiwan at the expense of the PRC, at least not in the foreseeable future.

In November 1992, however, the Japanese government made a significant gesture towards Taiwan. Chief Cabinet Secretary K. Kato met Shirley Kuo, who chaired Taiwan's Council for Economic Planning and Development, for an 'informal' discussion in Tokyo. It was the first cabinet-level meeting between Japanese and Taiwanese officials since Japan had restored relations with the PRC 20 years earlier. Encouraged by the recent move of several European countries to despatch cabinet ministers to Taiwan, Tokyo is reportedly keen to expand its non-official ties with Taipei, especially now that Taiwan and Russia have agreed to exchange trade representative offices and that the USA, in addition to the arms deal, is likely to review its semi-official ties with Taiwan.

Relations with the Republic of Korea   The ROK's decision in August 1992 to recognize the PRC had long been anticipated, but Taipei was disturbed enough by the action to talk seriously about retaliation, including economic sanctions. On 8 September it suspended air services between Taipei and Seoul.

For years Taiwan had tried hard to cement its relationship with the ROK, including expanding trade privileges and air service rights. Two-way trade in 1991 was US$3.1 billion, with the ROK becoming Taiwan's twelfth largest export partner and fifth largest source of imported goods. Taipei valued its Korean connection highly, not only because Seoul was Taipei's last and most long-standing formal diplomatic partner in Asia, but also because it is another divided nation fighting for reunification. During the Cold War years the two cooperated closely in resisting communist aggression and in resolving economic and social problems. The ROK was hostile to the PRC then, since the latter supported North Korea. Taiwan–ROK relations gradually began to change after 1973, when Seoul adopted an 'open-door' policy towards the PRC, and showed interest in forging ties.

However, the ROK made no breakthrough, except in some non-political activities, for the rest of the decade. Then, in 1983, the hijacking of a passenger plane from China triggered the first official contact between the two governments. The plane could only fly as far as Seoul, so the head of Chinese civil aviation flew there to negotiate the return of the aircraft. Diplomats from the two sides met in Tokyo. Seoul returned the plane and the passengers to China, but allowed the hijackers to go to Taiwan. These negotiations over the hijacking paved the way for a series of secret contacts between the two countries, for in the same year Seoul announced its 'northern diplomacy', one of the objectives being to normalize relations with Peking. It hoped to improve its ties with the Soviet Union and the PRC, and to balance those with the USA and Japan. The ROK–PRC normalization would also serve to counter Japan's role as the region's economic superpower, and to further isolate North Korea. Moreover the ROK had its eye on mainland China's huge market.

In 1985 Peking and Seoul were brought closer when the crew of a Chinese torpedo boat mutinied and sailed to South Korea. Secret negotiations for the ship's return were held in Hong Kong. From then on informal trade links began to grow. In 1988 the PRC took part in the Seoul Olympics, to the great chagrin of both Taiwan and North Korea. In June of that year the ROK government started to refer to the PRC as 'China' and to the ROC as 'Taiwan'. Direct trade and investment links between the ROK and the PRC gathered apace, especially when an export-processing zone was set up in northeast China, chiefly to attract the ROK's investment. In 1990 Seoul and Peking exchanged trade offices. The ROK trade mission in Peking was staffed with senior diplomats and was an embassy in all but name. Subsequently Taipei was on full alert and psychologically prepared for Seoul's diplomatic break.

Even so, when it did happen, Taipei reacted bitterly and criticized the ROK action as 'extremely unfriendly' and as exhibiting a 'lack of sincerity'. ROC Foreign Minister Frederick Chien commented: 'This whole case was full of betrayal and deceit.'[18] According to Taipei, whenever Taiwan's envoys had asked ROK leaders in recent years about rumours of ties being established with the PRC, they were always assured that the stories were groundless and that Taipei would be kept fully informed if and when negotiations with Peking took place. Thus from Taipei's point of view, Seoul had deliberately kept Taipei in the dark, while at the same time exploiting trade privileges with Taiwan.

This embarrassing defeat offered the DPP an excellent chance to attack the wisdom of the KMT's 'pragmatic diplomacy'. In the eyes of the DPP, the split with the ROK demonstrated the 'complete bankruptcy' of the KMT approach. At this stage there were suggestions in Taiwan of developing a rapport with North Korea, but after careful consideration this was ruled out.

However, there may be a political benefit for Taipei from Peking's recognition of the two Koreas. Previously the PRC had rejected dual recognition, but its rationale for opposing it appears to have been weakened by its acceptance of the formula 'one Korea, two governments'. Whether this will help Taiwan to promote its interest in dual recognition or dual representation remains to be seen. So far the ROK has failed to extract any concession from Peking over some kind of 'special relation' with Taiwan.

Relations with Western Europe

The so-called Taiwan problem is for Western Europeans no problem. There is only an island called Taiwan, which offers a very interesting business prospect. It is attracting even more attention since the PRC has made it clear that it does not object to European business activity in Taiwan if political overtones are excluded. Even the Vatican ... has great interests on the continent ... Any discussion of European perspectives concerning Taiwan, therefore, means speaking about European business interests on the island; political considerations about Taiwan and its future responses to international and regional development come into play insofar as these business interests may be threatened by any internal or external political event.[19]

Most Europeans do not know where Taiwan is: their only impression about Taiwan is that it is a place where cheap goods are made. They know very little about Taiwan's effort in democratization, about the emergence of a real opposition party... In contrast, people on Taiwan do not know very much about Europe.[20]

These observations are fairly characteristic of ROC–West European relations. In recent years, however, there has been a marked improvement.

Between 1950 and 1970 the ROC rated Western Europe as a low priority. Similarly Western Europe gave its contacts with Taipei the lowest profile possible to avoid irritating Peking. In 1974 Taipei took the initiative in promoting trade, economic, technological and cultural ties with Western Europe. Accordingly in 1975 it set up the Euro-Asia Trade Organization. This encouraged several European countries to establish trade offices in Taiwan, including the Anglo-Taiwan Trade Committee, the France-Asia Trade Promotion Association and Cultural Representation, and the Belgian Trade Association. In the meantime Taiwan had sent several 'Buy European' missions to Europe and held exhibitions of European goods in Taipei. It also set up commercial banking facilities in Europe. Two-way trade began to expand, with West Germany as the largest trading partner, followed by the United Kingdom, the Netherlands, France, Italy, Belgium, Sweden and Switzerland.

Since 1979 West European countries have begun to respond more enthusiastically to Taiwan's commercial appeal. There were several reasons for this change in attitude. First of all the Europeans were emboldened by the US AIT arrangement in Taiwan. Secondly, business transactions with Taiwan now have tacit approval from the PRC. Thirdly, Europeans were attracted by Taiwan's 'economic miracle'. Since 1991 they have taken an even greater interest in Taiwan because of its Six-Year Development Programme. It is said that a number of European countries have set their sights on Taiwan not only because of the lucrative profits to be had from the Programme, but also because 'they regard Taiwan as a spring-board to tap mainland China, Japan, Indochina and other Asian markets'.[21] Many European business people used to bypass Taiwan on visits to Japan and China. Since 1987 they have stopped over in Taiwan, having found the PRC to be a disappointing trade partner, and because Taiwan has improved the quality of its products. Finally, one should also note the decline of strategic considerations in Western Europe's China policy: that is, the PRC is no longer perceived as a strategic counterweight to the Soviet threat in Europe.

In 1989 France took the lead in upgrading its French Institute in Taipei, analogous to the US AIT. In 1991 the French Minister of Industry and Regional Planning, R. Fauroux, visited Taiwan privately. This visit broke the ban on European cabinet-level politicians visiting Taiwan. Since then more than 30 current ministers or former government leaders have been to Taiwan, including former West German Chancellor Helmut Schmidt, former French President Valéry Giscard d'Estaing, former French Prime Minister Michel Rocard and former British Prime Minister Margaret Thatcher.

Other visits were on a more official basis: by the Belgian Foreign Trade and Economics Minister in October 1992 (the first official visit since diplomatic ties were suspended in 1972); by the Austrian Economics Minister, also in October 1992 (the first official visit at ministerial level for 40 years); and by the Swiss Economic and Trade Delegation the following month (for the first time in 42 years). More significantly, in the same autumn Jürgen Möllemann, the Economics Minister and the Vice-Chancellor of Germany, became the first cabinet minister from that country to visit Taiwan. Bonn had previously kept Taiwan at a distance, and so Möllemann's visit marked a new official approval of contacts between the two countries. Indeed, he stressed the official nature of his visit, and also pushed the advantages of German technology for the projected high-speed train route between Taipei and Kaohsiung which was part of the Six-Year Programme. Furthermore, as the most senior cabinet minister to have visited Taiwan, Möllemann's visit indicated a positive change of attitude in Europe towards Taiwan.

By 1991 some 15 European countries had set up 18 'private' institutions in Taiwan for handling business and cultural exchanges and for facilitating technical cooperation. Some of the institutions, for instance the French, British, German and Spanish offices, are authorized to issue visas, thus upgrading substantive relations. They are headed by senior diplomats, usually 'on official leave', but sometimes even this formality is dispensed with. Meanwhile Taiwan has 20 such offices in 16 West European countries. Today there are 22 European banks with branches and representatives on the island. Five Taiwanese banks have opened similar offices in Europe. In the absence of diplomatic ties these offices have become very useful 'channels' in furthering economic, trade and financial ties between Western Europe and Taiwan.

Taipei's advances to Western Europe have also encountered a difficulty. Peking has protested about the growing number of Taipei's quasi-official contacts with European countries, especially regarding arms sales. In 1981 the Netherlands sold two submarines to Taiwan. Peking retaliated by downgrading diplomatic ties to the level of chargé d'affaires until 1984, when the Netherlands agreed to stop further sales. Taipei had considered this sale a breakthrough as it constituted the first political interaction with a European country since 1949. It also set a precedent, as more and more European countries have since attached less importance to Peking's political sensitivities. More recent European arms deals include the French decision to sell 6 frigates in 1990 (finalized in 1991, with the addition of 10 more vessels); the sale of torpedoes by Italy in the same year; the sale of rocket guidance and propulsion systems by the Belgian affiliate of the French firm Thomson CSF to the ROC air force; the contract with a German naval yard to build 4 minesweepers; and the French decision in November 1992 to sell 60 Mirage 2000 fighters, worth as much as US$4 billion, and at least a thousand short- and medium-range missiles to Taiwan. The PRC has protested about all these sales.

Peking has also been annoyed by Taipei's progress in developing air links with Europe. In 1983 Taipei exchanged air passenger services with Amsterdam. In retaliation the PRC banned KLM (which flies only to Hong Kong and not to any PRC mainland airport) from using Canton as an alternative airport. Currently Taipei has signed aviation agreements with Austria and Luxembourg. Similar agreements with Britain, France, Belgium, Ireland and Germany are under way.

Relations with the European Union   The evolution of the ROC's relations with West European countries reflects its relations with the EU, which has been building a barrier-free single market since 1993.

During the 1970s the EC seemed indifferent to the ROC. Not only was it unwilling to engage in political dialogue, but it was also discriminatory in trading terms. For instance, the EC had provided almost all Asian countries with the special treatment allowed by the Generalized System of Preferences. The only exception was Taiwan. This put Taiwanese products at a disadvantage.

The first official acknowledgment of the growing importance of trade with Taiwan came in 1985, when the European Parliament adopted a

'Resolution on Trade with Taiwan' at the suggestion of one of its members, J. Van Aerssen. This resolution, among other things, stressed Taiwan's economic relevance to Europe and the importance of taking every opportunity to develop trade contacts with it. Taiwan quickly seized the initiative and proclaimed 1986 the 'year of trade with Europe'. To follow this up, it sent several trade promotion groups to Europe. Nevertheless it was not until 1991 that the EC began to respond more enthusiastically. In June of that year 80 members of the European Parliament took the initiative in setting up the Association of Friends of Taiwan. Later in July the EC member states gave unanimous support to Taipei's GATT application. In November 1992 the European Parliament adopted new resolutions to strengthen ties with Taiwan. According to one resolution, the EC recognized Taiwan's important role in the international economy, and reaffirmed support for its bid for membership of GATT, the OECD and other international bodies. Yet it also stressed the continuity of the EC's 'one China' policy. And in May 1992 the Vice-President of the European Commission, Martin Bangemann, made a groundbreaking visit to Taiwan, as he was the first senior official to visit the island since the Community's establishment in 1957.

Relations with countries of the former Soviet bloc   The most remarkable adjustment in the ROC's foreign policy and external relations has been made in its approach to the former communist world. The ROC's short-term objective in this area is to cultivate substantive relationships with as many countries as possible. Its long-term goal is to upgrade such relations to a semi-official or official level. Such a dramatic switch, which would have been out of the question in previous decades, is a clear expression of Taipei's current flexibility and pragmatism.

It can also be argued that the ROC's previous rigidity was in part due to the unyielding external economic and trade practices of the communist countries. The ascendancy of Mikhail Gorbachev in the Soviet Union and the implementation of perestroika and glasnost brought about substantial reforms in the communist system. This development, together with Gorbachev's 1986 speech in Vladivostok calling for coexistence and better relations with Asian neighbours, including economic and trade cooperation with smaller capitalist societies such as the ROK and Taiwan, encouraged Taipei to make overtures to the former communist world.

Taiwan's approach to Eastern Europe began in 1979, when Taipei officially lifted its three decades of 'absolutely no contact' with several 'non-hostile' communist countries, including Poland, East Germany, Hungary, Yugoslavia and Czechoslovakia. Meanwhile it encouraged indirect trade with the Soviet Union, Bulgaria, Romania and Albania.

This approach began rather slowly, not only because the economic and trade activities of the communist countries were mainly under governmental control, but also because the lack of official and semi-official contacts between the two sides handicapped trade relations. For instance, it prevented the smooth handling of visa applications, commercial transportation, monetary remittances and the channels of communication indispensable for promoting trade and other commercial enterprises. In fact it was for political reasons that Taipei neither openly encouraged nor discouraged trade links with Eastern Europe during the 1980s.

After 1986 bilateral trade began to take off. By the late 1980s Hungary had become Taiwan's most important socialist partner, and trade increased rapidly after the collapse of communism in Europe. In 1990 Taiwan opened trade offices in Budapest and Prague. Similar types of institution are planned for Poland and Bulgaria. In order to develop these ties further, Taipei's Ministry of Foreign Affairs set up an Ad Hoc Committee on Eastern European Affairs in 1979. It also contributed US$10 million to the European Bank for Reconstruction and Development. At this stage Taipei officially included Eastern Europe as a focus for its 'pragmatic diplomacy'.

Two-way trade between Taiwan and Eastern Europe has continued to progress slowly, but more smoothly than at first. It constitutes, however, only a tiny fraction of Taiwan's total volume of trade. Practical difficulties, such as ideological dissimilarity, lack of legal protection, language and cultural differences, long-distance transport costs and still-rigid regulations dampened Taiwanese investment. In March 1992 Taipei signed an air services agreement with Bulgaria, the first with a former communist country, thus taking a step forward in its efforts to establish a global flight service network. The accord is expected to facilitate commercial and other civilian exchanges between Taiwan and other East European countries.

Relations with the Soviet Union opened up much later. Taipei began to gauge possible opportunities in Moscow shortly after Gorbachev became leader in 1985, but it was not until the Soviet Union disintegrated that Taipei decided to act.

In 1988 Taipei sent a six-man private trade mission to Moscow, Leningrad and Kiev, which included two government officials. This immediately sparked off a bitter debate within the KMT government.

The conservative faction, which since 1949 had dominated the ROC's anti-communist ideology and foreign policy, finally gave in and decided to accept the development of contacts. Since then Taiwanese business people, tourists, journalists and scholars have begun to pour in to what they had long thought of as the Iron Curtain countries, hoping to discover business opportunities and tourist attractions.

In May 1989 two Soviet officials arrived in Taipei for the Pacific Basin Economic Council (PBEC) meeting, the first 'official' visit. Later Taiwan dispatched a Soviet Markets Investigation Team to conduct a three-week fact-finding mission. In early 1990, amid reports of Soviet food shortages, Taiwan set up a cabinet-level task force to consider offering aid as a way to break the ice with its old communist enemy. Plans to send rice were put on hold, however, when Soviet troops intervened in the Baltic republics. Nevertheless, in the same year, Taiwan started to trade directly with the Soviet Union. Direct postal communication, direct investment and discussion on air links followed. Meanwhile 17 official Soviet delegations visited Taiwan for trade and other exchange purposes.

In the aftermath of the break-up of the Soviet Union in January 1992, the ROC's Vice-Foreign Minister, J. Chang, paid visits to several of the new republics. During this trip he made promises of US$15 million in medical aid to Ukraine and 100,000 tonnes of rice to Russia. Taipei also planned to exchange trade offices and bank branches, and to enhance economic and investment protection in Ukraine. This did not prevent subsequent arms deals between Ukraine and the PRC, nor between Russia and the PRC. However, following Russia's decision to resume government-to-government relations with the ROC, the establishment of the Moscow–Taipei Economic and Cultural Coordination Commission as permanent missions in Taipei and Kaohsiung, with counterparts in Moscow, St Petersburg and Vladivostok, is under way. These offices will technically be private since the two countries do not have diplomatic ties, but they will issue visas and their personnel will have diplomatic privileges. This opening with Russia has given Taipei hope of promoting similar relationships with Ukraine and Belarus.

Unfortunately Taipei missed the opportunity to establish formal ties with the Baltic republics as it hesitated to extend early recognition. Later Estonia, Latvia and Lithuania succumbed to the PRC threat to block their entry into the UN if they formalized relations with Taiwan. After Chang's visit in February 1992, Taipei set up consular ties with Latvia, a level of official relations just below formal diplomatic recognition. This was the first time Taipei had established such links with a country with which it did not have diplomatic ties. Taipei hopes that in time this 'Latvia model' could promote openings with other republics.

Relations with ASEAN nations No member of the Association of Southeast Asian Nations (ASEAN) established diplomatic ties with the PRC before 1974. Taipei was able to maintain limited substantive contacts, mainly in the form of agricultural assistance, with a number of these countries, including the Philippines (from 1964), Thailand (from 1969) and Indonesia (from 1976). Since 1985 common interests have drawn Taiwan and ASEAN together.

Taiwan wants to diversify its overseas markets, but more importantly it wants to use an economic card to promote its multifaceted interests. ASEAN is seen as a priority not only because it is geographically close to Taiwan and has a huge market, cheaper labour costs and ample natural resources, but also because it is a potential regional trading bloc with a large number of overseas Chinese. Most of the ASEAN countries need foreign investment, capital and technical expertise, and look to Taiwan's economic achievements as a model for their own development. In 1985 Taiwan began to develop transnational projects with the ASEAN nations; two-way trade between Taiwan and ASEAN, and Taiwanese investment in ASEAN have since grown steadily.

Gradually countries that formerly avoided any official contact have adopted a more friendly attitude towards Taiwan. This favourable situation has been further enhanced now that Taipei no longer insists that it is the sole legal government of all China. Since 1989 Taipei has formally acknowledged that ASEAN constitutes an essential component in its current flexible diplomacy. In 1991 Taipei declared an interest in becoming a non-regional ASEAN 'dialogue partner' as part of its efforts to strengthen mutual trade and economic cooperation and to increase the ROC's presence in the global community.[22] Later, in 1993, Taipei launched a bolder, more aggressive diplomacy 'towards the South'. Between 30 December 1993 and 5 January 1994 Premier Lian Chan went to Malaysia and Singapore for 'private holidays'. This 'holiday diplomacy' not only aimed at promoting Taiwan's commercial interests by diversifying trade away from the mainland, but also paved the way for President Lee Teng-hui's 'private holiday visits' to the Philippines, Indonesia and Thailand in February.

The ROC's relations with Singapore, in particular, can be taken as a prime example of Taipei's current flexibility. The ROC has never had diplomatic ties with Singapore, which became independent in 1965, and yet the two enjoy unusually close political, economic and military cooperation.

Until 1990, when Singapore finally extended recognition to the PRC, its China policy had been to maintain an equal distance between Taipei and Peking by recognizing neither and by having trade ties with both. Although this policy has been inconsistent with Taipei's concept of 'one China', Taiwan has decided to remain quiet on this issue because of broader ideological and economic interests. Over the years Premier Lee Kuan-yew (who retired in 1991) made some 20 visits, mostly unpublicized, to Taiwan and enjoyed a close friendship with President Chiang Ching-kuo and then with his successor President Lee. The latter's visit to Singapore in 1989, where he was referred to as the 'President from Taiwan' and received with full official honour, was of great significance. This state visit was made at a time when rumours of Singapore–PRC normalization were in the air. It thus indicated that Taipei had, in words and in deeds, departed from its historical burden of ideology and the 'one China' principle. Moreover it was the first state visit by a ROC President in twelve years, apparently the result of its policy of flexibility. After Singapore established formal ties with Peking, Singapore and the ROC continued their former semi-official ties.

Another unique aspect of the ROC–Singapore relationship has been military cooperation. For years Singapore – a city state without a hinterland – has sent military personnel to Taiwan for combat training, codenamed 'Starlight Project', which is a recognized operation among Southeast Asian countries. Moreover, it has been reported that the Singapore Navy has bought Taiwan-built vessels.

Since the 1980s the Philippines, too, has become increasingly important in Taipei's diplomacy. Despite the decision of President Ferdinand Marcos to break diplomatic ties with Taipei in 1975, relations have remained relatively stable, with military and security links continuing. Taipei is reported to train elements of the Philippine security forces at an army base in north-central Taiwan and sells to Manila substantial amounts of military equipment, including small arms, artillery, shells and ammunition.[23] The Philippines established an Asian Exchange Centre to replace its embassy in Taipei, with its counterpart, the Pacific Economic and Cultural Centre, opening in Manila. Both offices were granted certain diplomatic privileges and immunities. In 1989 they were renamed the Manila Economic and Cultural Office in Taipei and the Taipei Economic and Cultural Office in Manila.

Taipei's relations with Manila improved after the inauguration of President Corazon Aquino in 1986, when the Philippines were severely burdened by external debt and economic problems at home. In this context, Taipei has tried to use its economic muscle to establish a more official and diplomatic relationship. In 1988 Taipei overtook Japan and the USA as the Philippines' biggest foreign investor and its third largest trading partner. This is probably the most important factor in the upgrading of Taipei–Manila relations today.

Apparently the Philippine government values Taiwan's presence in its country. In July 1989 Manila set up an investment-processing centre in Taipei, to offer a 'one-stop-shop' service for Taiwanese businesses. Meanwhile it proposed a Philippines–Taiwan Beneficial Act to protect the legality of Taiwan's investment in the Philippines and further encourage it. This bill, modelled on the US–Taiwan Relations Act, has taken a very long time to pass through the Philippines' Congressional Committee system.

For years Peking has been annoyed by Manila's 'two-faced diplomacy'. Now Peking has threatened to break diplomatic ties with Manila should the bill be passed. Its concern is with the likely domino effect of the bill: 'The essence of the bill is to treat Taiwan as a country, to carry on official contact or contacts of an official nature with Taiwan, so as to upgrade the present relations between the Philippines and Taiwan.'[24] Peking's concern is not groundless. Frequent visits of high-ranking officials have taken place between Taipei and Manila, and even more irritating to Peking are Manila's occasional references to 'the ROC' in government statements.

In June 1992 the newly elected President, Fidel Ramos, said that he intended to improve Manila's ties with Taiwan: 'If the PRC can improve relations with Taiwan, why can't we?'[25] In August he openly proposed the joint development with Taiwan of Subic Bay naval base into a free-trade zone after US forces completed their withdrawal in December 1992. He also showed interest in paying a 'private' visit to Taiwan in the near future. In November the idea to develop the Bay jointly with Taiwan was put into effect when Taipei agreed to draft plans for a US$41 million industrial park there.

Relations with regional and international organizations When the ROC withdrew from the UN in 1971, the PRC's representatives promptly replaced those from Taiwan in the Security Council and other related bodies. The PRC's intention to squeeze Taiwan out of the international community was to a large extent successful. Nine years after the UN decision, the ROC's membership of international organizations had been reduced to only four specialized agencies, nine IGOs and 257 INGOs. Since 1988 Taipei has softened its previously uncompromising attitude and made every effort to join international organizations. Its flexibility can be seen in its relations with the International Olympic Committee (IOC), the Asian Development Bank (ADB), APEC and, currently, the GATT/WTO.

The ROC has been renamed 'Chinese Taipei' since 1979 in the IOC and 'Taipei, China' in the ADB since 1986. Later known as the 'Olympic formula' and the 'ADB formula' respectively, they have since been applied by other international bodies, especially NGOs, and have been found to work satisfactorily. The IOC solution enabled the ROC to participate in the 1984 Los Angeles Olympics and in the 1992 Barcelona Olympics. In the case of the ADB, the ROC continues to contest its forced change of name, but has decided to refrain from withdrawal: 'The benefit of remaining a participant in the ADB should be given priority over our concern for names and what they symbolise... Unless we break through this way of thinking, we are limiting our options in the international arena,' said a Taiwanese political scientist.[26]

The significance of the 'ADB formula' has been the flexible attitudes of both Peking and Taipei: Peking did not insist that Taiwan be ousted, while Taipei accepted the new name, albeit unwillingly, and became a co-member of the ADB with Peking. The 1988 ADB meeting was the first occasion on which the ROC and the PRC had both attended an IGO session. The ROC has since used the ADB to promote its interests of international visibility and 'dual representation'. In May 1989 Taiwan's Finance Minister, Shirley Kuo, went to Peking for an ADB meeting, the first official ministerial visit from Taiwan to the mainland for 40 years. Kuo's visit was considered a bold step in seeking *de facto* recognition of two separate political entities in China. It was also an acknowledgment of Taipei's planned return to the international community under the newly mooted 'one country, two governments' proposal. At the ADB annual meeting in 1992 Taipei again raised the hope of changing its name from 'Taipei, China' to 'Taipei China', since the latter formulation would signify an equal position *vis-à-vis* the PRC. Similarly Taipei floated several names under which it might be granted membership of APEC. Finally in 1991 it accepted the name 'Chinese Taipei' and joined simultaneously with the PRC and Hong Kong on an equal footing.

Taiwan's application to join GATT/WTO has received wide international attention. It applied in 1990 under the title of 'Taiwan, Penghu, Kinmen and Matsu Customs Territory' (TPKMCT), which indicated the areas under its effective control. Membership is extremely important to the ROC because, as a UN specialized agency, GATT/WTO would aid Taipei's attempts to join other international bodies and enable it to enjoy most-favoured-nation trade status in all of GATT's 107 member states. Furthermore, considering the ROC's peculiar 'non-state' status, GATT/WTO could act as a forum for settling trade disputes. In August 1992, under pressure from Peking, Taipei agreed to add 'Chinese Taipei' after TPKMCT as a sign of further flexibility. In November 1992, some 21 years after its withdrawal, the ROC was readmitted to GATT with observer status under the name 'TPKMCT, Chinese Taipei'. At present Taipei is attempting to join other important financial institutions, such as the World Bank, the OECD (which it joined in November 1995 as an observer) and the Montreal Protocol.

Currently Taipei is a member of 9 IGOs and 811 (mostly non-political) INGOs out of a total of 4,235.[27] The ADB, PBEC, PECC (Pacific Economic Cooperation Council) and APEC are the most important. The major obstacle to Taipei's relations with international organizations is still Peking. The fact that the PRC is a permanent member of the UN Security Council and is widely recognized as the legitimate government representing China has made the ROC's entry or re-entry to IGOs under its own name a very complicated political issue. The ROC cannot join any international organization which is political in nature and affiliated with the UN regardless of what name it takes. As Taiwan's Foreign Minister, Frederick Chien, pointed out: 'The ROC is caught in the dilemma of choosing between the real thing without the name, or the name without the real thing. It is hard to get both at the same time.'[28]

'Pragmatic diplomacy': assessment

Currently the ROC is recognized by 31 states, of which the largest is South Africa, and maintains active or '*de facto* non-political' or 'substantive relations' with some 150 countries and regions. It also has 80 representative offices in 51 countries with no diplomatic ties with the ROC. Among them, 13 offices use the official name of the ROC.[29] In European countries most of the ROC's offices have now been renamed so as to include the word 'Taipei', which makes them more recognizable and is also a sign of upgraded status (e.g. the Taipei Representative Office in London). To date more than 30 countries which do not have diplomatic relations with the ROC have set up over 35 representative offices, associations or visa-issuing centres (most of these offices accept visa applications), and the number is increasing.

Viewed from this perspective the 'pragmatic diplomacy' has produced tangible results. The ROC today is no longer totally isolated, and the situation is better than it was during the 1970s, when many Taiwanese still felt set apart from the world and suffered an international identity crisis, and when many foreign countries considered the ROC a passing phenomenon and hesitated to make contacts with it. Over the years Taiwan's increasing wealth, growing record of democratization, political and social stability, and pragmatic emphasis on building bilateral trade relationships have put it back on the world stage. Now it is aiming for membership of major global organizations. It has rejoined GATT and the OECD as an observer and later expects to join the World Bank and the Montreal Protocol. Eventually it hopes to win back at least observer status at the UN – a long-term goal clearly stated in the ROC *Foreign Policy Report*, published on 21 January 1993. Its foreign policy is no longer reactive but more and more proactive, and the emerging new international order seems – at least provisionally – to have provided a favourable environment for the conduct of the ROC's unorthodox diplomacy.

The effectiveness of the 'pragmatic diplomacy' may be assessed according to its declared objectives to: (1) consolidate existing ties and establish new ones; (2) upgrade substantive relations with countries with no diplomatic ties; and (3) join or rejoin international organizations.

Consolidation and establishment of diplomatic ties

First, how far has Taiwan established or re-established diplomatic ties? Since 1989 it has established diplomatic ties with ten countries. Except for Nauru, all these countries had previously had diplomatic ties with the PRC. The case of Grenada is of particular significance as for a time it set the precedent for dual recognition. At present Taipei's diplomatic connections are concentrated in Africa, Latin America and the South Pacific. Most of them want aid from Taipei. Liberia, for example, was attracted mainly by Taiwan's donation of some 15,000 tonnes of rice. Similarly Niger was attracted by a generous promise of technical and financial aid. In this regard the ROC's diplomatic achievements are not solidly based, as some aid recipients might revert to links with Peking if the latter offered a more attractive package.

Since the USA introduced its new China policy in 1979, the ROC has suffered diplomatic setbacks. The Ivory Coast switched recognition to the PRC in 1983, Uruguay did so in 1988, Saudi Arabia in 1990 and the ROK in 1992. Taipei also lost Lesotho in 1983, recovered it in 1990, and lost it again in December 1993. The loss of Saudia Arabia was particularly dispiriting because it had been a long-term anti-communist ally of the ROC, the only state in the Middle East officially to recognize Taipei, and also its principal oil supplier. Since then the Middle East has become a relatively weak spot in the ROC's foreign relations network, although the break with Saudi Arabia did make possible the exchange of representative offices with Israel. Similarly the loss of the ROK has left a void for the ROC in Asia. Even though Taiwan is now internationally recognized as 'too rich to be ignored', it is still diplomatically isolated among the economic powers of the Pacific rim. It is evident, therefore, that despite recent gains the ROC is actually losing ground in terms of formal diplomacy. It has failed to prevent Indonesia, Singapore, Brunei, Israel and the newly independent republics of the former Soviet Union from formalizing diplomatic ties with the PRC.

Promotion of non-diplomatic ties

How successful has 'pragmatic diplomacy' been? Clearly it has brought some success in promoting non-diplomatic relations. Relations with Western Europe have improved substantially, as have those with the ASEAN nations. Other breakthroughs include relations with Russia, Latvia, Ukraine, Portugal, Iceland, Angola, India, Israel and Outer Mongolia. Most significant has been the resumption of US arms sales to Taiwan, as well as the French Mirage deal. Meanwhile Taiwan has strengthened bonds in its own region. It now conducts intensive trade and commercial activities in Vietnam, the Philippines, Malaysia, Thailand and Indonesia, and it has become a leading investor there. It has also increased aid to the region.

In some ways Taiwan now sees itself as a balancing force between the PRC and neighbouring countries. Vietnam, for example, with its historical fear of Chinese hegemony, has opened its doors to US$755 million in Taiwanese investment, the largest amount from any country. Saigon and Taipei resumed direct air links in September 1992, and Taipei has plans to provide Saigon with US$15 million in aid. In the absence of diplomatic ties Taipei has signed several 'investment guarantee agreements' to protect its investments and economic interests abroad. Vietnam has been the first socialist country to sign such an agreement with Taiwan. Others have since been signed with a further six countries: the USA,

Singapore, Indonesia, the Philippines, Paraguay and Panama. Negotiations are under way with Turkey, South Africa, Nicaragua, Latvia, Russia, Belarus, Ukraine and Malaysia. And the range of countries which can be visited by Taiwanese leaders has widened. Apart from visits to the Southeast Asian countries mentioned above, in May 1994 President Lee went to Costa Rica, South Africa and Swaziland. It was the first visit of this kind for 17 years. In June 1995 Premier Lien Chan made an official visit to the Czech Republic, despite furious protests from Peking. And in the same month President Lee made a 'private' visit to his alma mater, Cornell University, in the USA.

Evidently 'pragmatic diplomacy' has its merits, but it cannot work miracles. Moreover, unofficial and non-political economic, cultural and social ties, however practical and numerous, can never be a substitute for formal relations. As most of the representative offices are 'private' institutions, Taiwan encounters enormous handicaps when handling issues such as arms purchases: namely, the prolonged hesitation of the USA and other Western countries to commit themselves to sales of military weapons or to cooperation on military technology. Similarly Japan was unwilling to go through 'official channels' to resolve problems over its trade surplus with Taiwan. In this respect 'pragmatic diplomacy' has its limits in terms of protecting Taipei's basic national interests: another good example is the ROK's 'disloyalty' in recognizing the PRC, having benefited from contacts with Taiwan for many years. Worst of all, no matter what Taiwan does, its room for manoeuvre is severely constrained by the PRC. Any country that befriends Taipei risks retaliation from Peking. In 1991 alone 20 countries, including Poland, Hungary, the Philippines, Malaysia and the Soviet Union, were forced to reaffirm that 'the PRC is the sole legal government of China, and Taiwan is part of China'. When Niger and Latvia established ties with Taipei, Peking punished them by severing its own links. Needless to say, Peking reacted bitterly to the US and French aircraft deals with Taiwan and warned of 'serious consequences'.

Thus the ROC's intention to translate its substantive relations into a higher level of semi-official or official interaction still seems premature. It is extremely unlikely that major trading powers such as the USA, Western Europe or Japan would extend recognition to the ROC at the expense of the PRC. Rather, they intentionally keep Taiwanese officials at arm's length. Despite the weapons deals and several other breakthroughs, most countries continue to recognize the PRC as the major power that it is. Likewise, most of the former communist-bloc countries would prefer to continue close political collaboration with Peking, while exploring economic opportunities with Taiwan. Thus Russian President Boris Yeltsin commented that his decision to establish ties with Taiwan would not change his government's long-held 'one China' policy. This premise obviously sets a limit on the future development of Russia's relations with Taiwan. A similar statement was made by the German Economics Minister during his 'official' visit to Taiwan in November 1992.

Finally the stability of the ROC's substantive relations cannot be fully guaranteed. Taiwan's improving external relations are based on its economic strength and import-export trade. Were Taiwan's economy to encounter negative growth so that it could no longer support substantial levels of trade, such ties might be undermined or even terminated. It should also be remembered that the PRC is now slowly joining the ranks of the Asian 'tigers'. In the long run its economy, based on 1.2 billion people, will overshadow Taiwan's 20 million, no matter how hard the latter work. Taiwan may slowly lose its economic advantage over the mainland in the conduct of foreign affairs.

Links with international organizations

How successful has Taiwan been in entering or re-entering international organizations? Despite Peking's interference, Taipei has managed to gain entry to several regional bodies, such as the ADB, APEC and PECC. More important has been Taiwan's readmittance to GATT as an observer – the doors of the IGOs are now slowly opening. Taipei hopes that this will provide a partial guarantee for its future security, by facilitating economic activity and enhancing national prestige and international visibility. Ultimately it may be able to regain a place in international society, but there is still a long way to go. As Taiwan's Foreign Minister openly admitted: 'A hundred minutes of effort on our part may just equal Peking's one minute of effort.'[30]

External influences

The ROC's current frustration in international diplomacy can be seen, in retrospect, as the combined result of policy changes in the USA, Japan and other countries during the 1970s, of the concomitant changes in the international political environment during the same period, of Peking's continuous efforts at diplomatic isolation of the ROC, and of the ROC's own uncompromising diplomacy until the late 1980s. It is the last two factors which will play the larger part in shaping the future direction of the ROC's diplomacy and its future status.

To gain diplomatic leverage the KMT government has softened its previous uncompromising attitude towards the PRC and has since 1987 improved relations considerably. However, as long as the PRC remains intransigent on the 'one China, two systems' proposal and continues to block the ROC internationally, Taipei has little chance of improving its world status. As long as most countries acknowledge the PRC as an important international force and want to maintain good relations with it, the effectiveness of the 'pragmatic diplomacy' will be limited. Nor is it helped by opposition from the DPP inside Taiwan, as described in Chapter 2.

Security

Finally, 'pragmatic diplomacy' can also be evaluated from the security standpoint. The fact that the ROC has now forged more external contacts, enjoys a better international reputation and is accepted as a viable economic reality seems to have helped its development and security. However, the increasing trend of economic, social and cultural contacts between a small Taiwan and a huge mainland, since Taiwan's opening to the mainland in 1987, poses a new security threat to Taiwan: the danger of political, economic and social absorption by the PRC.

As the PRC's economy booms and political tensions between the rival governments in Taipei and Peking ease, billions of US dollars are being channelled out of Taiwan for investment on the mainland. This large-scale investment, which began in the late 1980s, has accelerated as Taiwan's economy has become more closely interlinked with that of the PRC. A large, sustained capital outflow would have a negative effect on Taiwan's economy. In fact, Taiwan's stock and property markets have already been affected. Two-way trade reached US$5.7 billion in 1991, more than double the 1988 figure of US$2.7 billion. By 1992 Taiwanese investment on the mainland already totalled US$10 billion, twice what it had been the previous year. It is estimated that Taiwanese operate some 3,000 companies on the mainland.

This development has caused concern among some senior government officials in Taiwan. They have warned that economic ties with the mainland may be 'overheating'. Unless the government can find ways to encourage domestic investment, ever more manufacturing could move to the mainland in the coming years, and so measures have been proposed to restrict investment. Another, more serious, consequence of the huge Taiwanese investment on the mainland is the risk of 'nationalization' by the PRC government. Since Taiwan and the mainland are still technically at war, there is as yet no legal protection for Taiwan's investment there. Furthermore, intensive people-to-people contact has highlighted Taiwan's vulnerability. From November 1987 to the middle of 1992 nearly four million people from Taiwan visited the mainland, while 30,000 visitors from the mainland came to Taiwan. And the trend is increasing. Hence the fear of dependence and finally political absorption on the PRC's terms.

It is clear, then, why ROC foreign policy has given top priority to gaining international recognition and admission to international organizations such as the UN. In 1993 Taiwanese efforts to re-enter the UN had won support from seven Latin American countries: Nicaragua, Costa Rica, Guatemala, Paraguay, Panama, the Solomon Islands and St Christopher. They wrote to the UN Secretary-General appealing for consideration to be given to the issue of Taiwanese representation. They were supported in the General Assembly by a further 23 countries, three of which (Singapore, the Ivory Coast and Uruguay) have no official ties with Taiwan. In 1994 the number of UN members supporting Taiwan increased to 26, and seven of these (Jordan, Latvia, the Czech Republic, the Philippines, Fiji, Belgium and Papua New Guinea) had no diplomatic ties with Taiwan. However, on neither occasion did the question reach the official agenda of the General Assembly. This came as no surprise to Taiwan. 'It took the PRC some twenty years to enter the UN,' some government officials openly declared. 'We can wait for an equally long time.'

The recent arms race along the Taiwan Straits has provided the DPP with an excellent chance to challenge the KMT government's mainland policy, as Peking has shown no 'friendly response' to Taipei's policy of goodwill and has not renounced the use of force to conquer Taiwan. Whatever the motivation for the US F-16 decision, Taiwan's economic wealth, its flexible diplomacy, and the current more favourable international environment made the deal possible. The same was true for the French Mirage deal. Taiwan had been trying for years to buy advanced jet fighters but the US and French governments previously refused to sell for fear of offending Peking. Taipei's approach to other Western countries, including Germany, the Netherlands and Israel, also failed for the same reasons. Thus Taiwan had been forced to rely upon primitive 1960s jets – F-5Es and F-104s – types which have suffered many crashes. In view of the security threat posed by the PRC, and the uncertain development of relations along the Taiwan Straits, the US and the French arms sales have definitely strengthened Taiwan's defence capability. The new aircraft will give Taiwan's military greater credibility as a deterrent force and will boost the morale of Taiwan's armed forces. Meanwhile, as one author observed, the drawdown of European military establishment and competition among defence industries for foreign sales has left the door open for additional arms purchases by Taiwan, including more Mirage fighters. Military planners in Taiwan would also like to augment the navy's two operational submarines and build a small submarine force of up to ten boats.[31]

Peking is said to be seriously upset by the arms sales to Taiwan, but there seems little it can do in retaliation for the time being. One reason for this is that the USA is such an important trading partner. Another reason is that Peking cannot afford to retaliate simultaneously against two major Western powers – relations with the UK are strained over Hong Kong. 'It is one thing for Taipei to play "money diplomacy" with the Nigers and Belizes and even the Latvias of the world,' said a European diplomat in Peking, 'but Peking might well worry when Taiwan's deep pockets and capital investment plans earn it the courtship of France, Germany, Australia, the USA, Israel, Russia – all the big-time players in a recession-hit world.'[32] Thus Taiwan's diplomatic success may paradoxically create greater uncertainty over its security.

Notes

1 Both Dutch and German shipyards are apparently willing to sell Taiwan diesel-powered submarines if their governments permit it. Negotiations have reportedly taken place for the purchase of new submarines or a technology-transfer arrangement that would allow the China Ship-Building Corporation in Kaohsiung to build the boats in Taiwan. The Dutch would probably have done a deal already, were it not that they hoped for a bigger Fokker aircraft deal with Peking.

2 *Far Eastern Economic Review (FEER)*, 3 December 1992, pp. 8–10.

3 *International Herald Tribune (IHT)*, 27 April 1987, p. 6.

4 *Lien-ho pao (United Daily News, UDN)*, 23 September 1992, p. 2; *FEER*, 12 November 1992, pp. 16–22.

5 *UDN*, 11 March 1992, p. 2.

6 *The China Times*, 8 July 1988, p. 11.

7 Ibid.

8 *Asian Weekly* (Taipei, in Chinese), 2 April 1989, p. 2.

9 Interview with the Japanese *Yomiuri Shimbun* on 8 May 1989. See *The China Times*, 9 May 1989, p. 1.

10 Frederick Chien, 'The Republic of China under the New International

Order in the Post-Cold War Era' (speech delivered at the International Conference on the Republic of China and the New International Order, 21 August 1991, Taipei); and his 'Report to the Legislative Yuan: Current International Situation and the ROC's Diplomatic Strategy', 29 October 1990, Taipei.

11 For more details, see G. Chan, 'Sino-Vatican Diplomatic Relations: Problems and Prospects', *China Quarterly*, 120 (December 1989), pp. 814–36.

12 Y.S. Wang (ed.), *Foreign Policy of the Republic of China on Taiwan: An Unorthodox Approach* (New York: Praeger, 1990), p. 39.

13 *IHT*, 4 December 1992, p. 15.

14 *IHT*, 5–6 September 1992, p. 5.

15 *UDN*, 23 May 1992, p. 5.

16 *Chung-yang jih-pao* (*Central Daily News*, *CDN*), 24 May 1990, p. 2.

17 Ibid.

18 *FEER*, 3 September 1992, p. 10.

19 R. Drifte, 'European and Soviet Perspectives on Future Responses in Taiwan to International and Regional Development', *Asian Survey*, November 1985, p. 111.

20 Wang (ed.), *Foreign Policy*, p. 140.

21 *The China Post* (Taipei), 19 December 1991, p. 18.

22 *The China Post*, 17 December 1991, p. 9.

23 *FEER*, 20 March 1986, p. 17.

24 Wang (ed.), *Foreign Policy*, p. 90.

25 *UDN*, 14 June 1992, p. 1.

26 *UDN*, 16 August 1992, p. 2, and 18 August 1992, p. 1.

27 The IGOs include Interpol, the International Committee of Military Medicine, the International Cotton Advisory Committee, the International Office of Epizootics, the Asia Productivity Organization, the Afro-Asian Rural Reconstruction Organization, the Asia and Pacific Council, the International Union for the Publication of Customs and Tariffs and the Permanent Court of Arbitration.

28 H.C. Wei, 'Opening Doors to International Organizations', *Sinorama* (Taipei), vol. 17, no. 1 (January 1992), p. 85.

29 These include Argentina, Bahrain, Bolivia, Ecuador, Fiji, Kuwait, Libya, Madagascar, Mauritius, Nigeria, Papua New Guinea, United Arab Emirates and Zaire.

30 *UDN*, 14 April 1992, p. 1.

31 *FEER*, 3 December 1992, p. 9.

32 Ibid., p. 10.

Chapter 5

Conclusion

Peter Ferdinand

In few states of the world have international economic and political trends diverged as much as on Taiwan since the late 1980s. There are increased pressures both to look outwards and to look inwards. On the one hand the growth of Taiwan's economy has led to prosperity and an increasingly outward orientation. Taiwan is increasingly integrated into the world economy and wishes to become better integrated into world organizations, such as the WTO and the UN, so that it can enhance its prestige and defend its economy.

On the other hand, its political development, the process of democratization, requires greater attention to domestic moods and priorities than the government was wont to pay before 1987. That has meant that the political system on Taiwan can now be seen to be more legitimate than ever before. Previously martial law kept the rift between the minority ruling 'mainlanders' and the majority 'Taiwanese' under control. The dogma that the government on Taiwan was really that of the whole of China was a vital element in the government's self-legitimization, and ensured that the KMT remained in power. No serious evidence suggested that significant numbers of Taiwanese citizens wanted reunification with communist China on the latter's terms, but that did not mean that the system on Taiwan was felt to be legitimate by most of its citizens. Now, however, they are prepared to take an active part in elections, and do not disrupt national life to protest about the outcome. The waves of labour unrest which swept through Taiwan in the aftermath of the lifting of martial law have now subsided. Although there may still be some unresolved constitutional issues, there is a general acceptance of the rules of the system and a feeling that it can be made to reflect the people's wishes.

Yet this greater sensitivity on the part of the government to domestic concerns paradoxically also led to its campaign to rejoin the UN. The KMT leadership under President Lee Teng-hui felt it needed a dramatic foreign policy success to impress domestic voters and pre-empt criticism from the opposition DPP. Because of its diplomatic marginality, the government possibly overestimated the extent to which sympathetic governments would support it in the UN, or indeed the power they had to influence the PRC, a permanent member of the Security Council, into giving way. They certainly underestimated the vehemence of the response of the PRC once roused.

This also reflected a more general realization by the Taiwanese government that economic success has made the problems of government, both domestically and internationally, more, not less, complex. Although money can facilitate some solutions to policy problems, the government also needs to become more sophisticated, better able to devise comprehensive solutions to complex problems. During the 1980s it began to appreciate this fact domestically, especially in the latter half of the decade, ironically a time when the country was experiencing unexpected growth in exports again after the revaluation of the yen. Yet the effect was an explosion in urban land prices, a widening of income disparities, and the launch of costly public-works projects which then caused enormous dislocation. The apparently never-ending series of problems, with disruption to the lives of millions, caused by the construction of the Taipei underground railway was a particularly graphic symbol of this weakness, but it was not unique. The miscalculations of the Six-Year Development Programme, and the abortive negotiations first with McDonnell Douglas and then with British Aerospace over large projects for aerospace collaboration, showed the same limitation. Solutions to large-scale problems cannot simply be bought.

To some extent the same problem bedevils Taiwan's foreign relations. For 30 years it has been practising chequebook diplomacy – trying to win the support of nations through offers of assistance. Before 1971 such a diplomatic strategy made sense. As long as the ROC occupied the Chinese seat at the UN and in the Security Council, Taiwanese aid to Third World countries helped to ensure that the issue of PRC membership did not get on to the UN's agenda. And since all states at the UN have equal votes irrespective of size, aid to small countries had the effect of maximizing the ROC's diplomatic leverage. Since 1971, however, support from Third World countries has made – and can make – no significant difference to the ROC's global diplomatic position. Above all, the PRC's permanent membership of the Security Council and its veto powers ensure that Taiwan cannot 'return' to the UN, however many other countries vote for it. That the Taiwanese government should continue to offer useful assistance projects to the developing world is entirely laudable, but it is unlikely to serve the fundamental goal of international recognition – at least, unless and until the UN rules establishing the prerogatives of permanent members of the Security Council are changed.

What continues to obstruct Taiwan's foreign policy, as well as its economy, is the unresolved relationship with the mainland. Even the strategy for orienting the economy towards providing services for international business in the Asia-Pacific region as an 'international operations centre' is threatened by hostilities from across the Taiwan Straits. Multinational corporations will be reluctant to buy heavily into such a concept unless they can be assured of long-term stability.

The prospects for a complete, peaceful resolution of the dispute with the mainland are still remote. Here, too, the political and economic trends are contradictory. On the one hand the economies of the two Chinas are converging. Taiwan's increasing trade with and investment in the mainland will be accentuated after reversion of Hong Kong to China in 1997. However much the Taiwanese government tries to discourage businesses from setting up shop on the mainland for fear of increasing the country's dependence on the PRC, it will be frustrated by contrary domestic considerations. Businesses are motivated by the need to make profits, and domestic production on Taiwan has become much less competitive internationally since the 1980s across a whole range of sectors, particularly the labour-intensive ones, as domestic costs of labour and land have risen dramatically. So factory-owners have increasingly opted to produce abroad where costs are lower. For the present, and probably for some considerable time to come, the PRC will be an attractive option for them.

In general, what has happened so far, as was mentioned in Chapter 3, is that Taiwanese businesses have exported outdated plant to the mainland where it can continue to make profits when operated by cheaper labour. But the main trend of economic relationships with the mainland will be likely to take a different form in the future. Increasingly, as was also suggested in Chapter 3, Taiwanese companies will develop into high-quality, high-cost manufacturers, needing supplies of semi-finished goods and components. The same has been true of Japanese companies. In the case of Taiwan, these supplies will come increasingly from the mainland. It is true that this will also mean that to a certain extent the mainland will become more dependent on Taiwan. But the share of the mainland's exports going to Taiwan will be much smaller than the share of Taiwan's exports going to the mainland. There will be increasing interdependence, but it will continue to be skewed in the mainland's favour.

After 1997 there will no longer be any point in insisting that trade with the mainland should take place via Hong Kong, so that there are no direct links. It will not take long for direct shipping and air links to develop. Indeed the infrastructure for such developments is already being built on both sides of the Straits, and the Taiwanese government has proposed that a trans-shipment zone should be established on the island for goods which are being transported to the mainland from abroad.

The Taiwanese government's ability to dissuade or even prevent its businesses from investing on the mainland will also be undermined by the rival trends of macroeconomic liberalization. The government will be under pressure to reduce its interventions in the economy not only from its own companies but also from developed nations, which will expect this as a condition for membership of international economic organizations such as the WTO and, conceivably, the OECD. Thus control of domestic economic activity by the Taiwanese state will decline. This will be intensified by the prospect of both Chinas joining the WTO. In theory both states should extend MFN status to each other, although they could be exempted from this on the grounds of security. Nevertheless, once this dual entry takes place, the likelihood is that it will further encourage cross-Straits trade.

In so far as the government achieves success in its own attempts in the 1990s to encourage foreign investment on the island by multinational companies wishing to use Taiwan as an operations centre for the Asia-Pacific region, the most likely outcome is an increase in economic links with the mainland. Why should multinational companies wish to locate on Taiwan to do business with Southeast Asia, when they can do so from Singapore, which already has a better transport and communications infrastructure, or Kuala Lumpur, which is building one? What Taiwan can offer is access to the mainland and expertise in doing business with mainland Chinese companies.

For these reasons, then, the prospects are for increasing dependence upon the mainland China market. Politically, however, the trends point in the opposite direction. As Chapter 2 showed, there is a growing self-confidence among the Taiwanese population, who expect greater international recognition for their economic and political achievements, and who also are concerned about the possible costs for Taiwan of reunification with the mainland when the latter is so much poorer, at least on a per capita basis. Politically this has found expression in the rise of the DPP as the chief opposition party, with its aim of an independent Taiwan.

It does not necessarily follow that there is a growing constituency for independence for Taiwan. Public opinion polls on the island continue to show that only 15–30 per cent of the population would support that. As was shown in Chapter 2, membership of the DPP is scarcely greater than that of the New Party, let alone the Kuomintang. But it does mean that large numbers of people are sceptical about reunification in the foreseeable future, and that scepticism has been articulated by President Lee Teng-hui. In a speech to mark National Day on Taiwan in October 1995, he said that Taiwan would seek reunification with the mainland only after China had raised its level of democratization and its living conditions to become much closer to those of Taiwan.

Per capita income on the mainland in 1992, using measures of dollar comparability rather than purchasing power parity, was US$470 and on Taiwan, $10,202. Even if we assume that the PRC economy continues to grow in the indefinite future at 9 per cent annually – the rate the PRC government has recently declared to be its target for the next Five-Year Plan – it would take 35 years for the average per capita income on the mainland to reach the present level of Taiwan's. But in the meantime the Taiwanese economy would have continued to grow too. If we assume an average figure for Taiwan of 4 per cent, i.e. quite high by developed-country standards but still lower than the average over the past 40 years or indeed the past 5 years, then per capita income there would have reached over US$40,000 in 35 years' time. In other words, the disparity between the averages of the two states at the same time would have fallen from 1:20 to 1:4, but it would still be substantial. Thus if President Lee's precondition for considering reunification were strictly adhered to, it would be the middle of the next century before the issue could be put on the agenda even on economic grounds. And that leaves entirely open the separate question of political convergence, which he also mentioned. How far would the political system on the mainland have democratized in that time?

It is easy to see why the mainland's leadership is sceptical about President Lee's desire for reunification. In turn it has led to increasingly savage attacks upon him personally, and to the mainland's two 'tests' of missiles into the sea near Taiwan in July and August 1995. It was a reminder of the possibility that the mainland might use military force to take Taiwan if the latter did declare independence. This seriously excited the public on Taiwan, although it did not lead to panic.

In fact, it is not likely that the mainland will use force to settle the dispute. For one thing, the distance across the Taiwan Straits is around 100 miles and the Taiwanese defence forces would be able to mount a spirited defence. For another thing, the PRC would not be able to launch a surprise attack. It would take enormous planning and lengthy preparation, as well as the massing of troops in Fukien province. This could not escape observation by reconnaissance satellites, especially those of the USA. Under the terms of the Taiwan Relations Act, the President is obliged to report to Congress any threat to Taiwan within 90 days of becoming aware of it. That in itself would ensure that the information became public, with governments around the world being forced by their media to respond.

Consequently, however much the PRC asserts that relations with Taiwan are a matter solely for the Chinese to resolve, they would necessarily become an international issue. Three of the five Permanent Members of the UN Security Council (the USA, France and Russia) have recently supplied advanced equipment either to a fourth – the PRC – or to Taiwan. Resupplies during any conflict or confrontation might well become an issue at the Security Council. Even if other countries were unwilling to commit themselves to defending Taiwan, many governments would find themselves under pressure from public opinion to try to restrain the PRC from crushing a democratic state. The ghosts of Tiananmen Square would be resurrected. Multinational corporations, too, would be nervous about the impact on their businesses on Taiwan and would press their own governments for reassurance. Even if the PRC limited itself to a naval blockade, that would still be very damaging to those businesses.

Thus well before the PRC was capable of launching an overwhelming attack, it would find itself under enormous diplomatic pressure to pull back. Even countries in East Asia which would rather avoid entanglement in any dispute would be nervous about the implications for East Asian security of a triumphant, even a triumphalist PRC. Moreover, the confidence of foreign investors in the stability of market reforms in the PRC and in the acceptance by the leadership there of the benefits of international integration would take a serious beating.

For all these reasons, then, any attempt at settlement of the Taiwan issue through force could not remain a matter solely for the Chinese, even if no other country were willing to contribute military force.

Other countries must recognize that they will be called upon to take a stand if conflict threatens across the Straits, even if they wish to avoid becoming involved militarily. Whether or not the threat of military action becomes a reality, the issue of ROC–PRC relations has gained a higher profile than in the 1980s. Even if other countries continue to avoid taking sides, they will not find it so easy simply to base their policies upon the declaration in the Shanghai Communiqué that there is one China and that its government is located in Peking.

All of this means that, in policy terms, countries in other parts of the world must begin to treat the PRC, Hong Kong and Taiwan as part of a whole, for within certain limits the leaders of those three entities already do so. Even though recent talk about a 'Greater Chinese Economic Space' is premature, not least because of the political obstacles, it is becoming less and less sensible to pursue separate policies towards each part of the triangle.

The mainland's relations with Taiwan now figure on the domestic political agenda of the leadership in Peking. Equally, the return of Hong Kong to the mainland and the ways in which it is treated by the mainland also figure on the agenda of political leaders on Taiwan. Since the government in Taipei agrees with the view of the UK government and the Governor of Hong Kong that the recent changes in the method of election to the Legislative Council there do not contravene the Joint Declaration signed by the UK and the PRC in 1984, it will watch with particular attention how the Council is treated by Peking. If it is dissolved and members are replaced by Peking appointees, people on Taiwan will be likely to conclude that any reunification agreement they might sign with Peking could well suffer the same fate, even if it expressly laid down the right of the Taiwanese to retain their own, more democratic system. They will draw the same conclusion if the legal system, the police and the civil service in Hong Kong come to be subverted.

So policy towards Taiwan can be devised only within a more general scheme of policy towards the PRC and Hong Kong. In turn, the prerequisite for an overall policy towards these three entities is a view about China's future place in East Asian and indeed global relations.

If the rest of the world needs to re-examine its policies towards China, Taiwan and Hong Kong, the people on Taiwan also need to rethink their relations with the rest of the world. Taiwan has made enormous strides since 1949. It is the twelfth largest trading nation in the world, and it has the twentieth largest economy. It now also leads the way in democratization in the Chinese world. Its achievements are a justifiable source of pride for its population. Understandably they believe that the rest of the world should accord them greater attention and stop treating them with disdain or embarrassment.

They are also in the process of re-evaluating their own identity. In part that is an understandable reaction against the years when schools on Taiwan taught virtually nothing about the history of the peoples who had lived there. Those who come from generations of inhabitants on the island – the majority – quite rightly feel that more attention should be devoted to these issues. It is a filial, in a way a Confucian, demand. In the process they also wonder how far they are truly 'Chinese'.

Naturally they have different historical traditions from the rest of China. Living on an island somewhat distant from the mainland, their orientation has traditionally been towards the sea, the horizon and whatever lies beyond it. They have a longer tradition of dealings with non-Chinese, and so they have a certain cosmopolitanism, strengthened by business experience since 1949. As Taiwan was part of the Chinese state for at most three hundred years, and as much of the population or their ancestors fled there to escape from disorders or persecution on the mainland, they share a refugee culture with the people of Hong Kong. Many have a more sceptical view of the glorious civilization of the Middle Kingdom. They speak Chinese dialects which are found only in the south of Fukien province across the Straits, so their identification with the more distant parts of China is tenuous. More recently they were subjected to 50 years of Japanese colonial rule, and although this was a brutal regime, over time some Taiwanese learnt to live with it. President Lee himself once confessed that until the age of 20 he felt more Japanese than Chinese or Taiwanese. More recently still, Taiwan's economic success since 1949 has developed a set of middle-class values, which are at odds with the 'socialist' ethos of the PRC. Now its democratic system both adds to the sense of difference and provides channels for articulating it.

So the question the people on Taiwan are collectively addressing is whether they are *qualitatively* different from Chinese on the mainland. Actually they are far from united in their response, as is only to be expected given their diversity of backgrounds and life experiences. Before 1949 even Taiwanese whose ancestors came from Fukien province were split between those from Changchou and those from Ch'uanchou counties. Then after 1949 the division between 'mainlanders' and 'Taiwanese' was laid over this. More recently, as the latter distinction has declined in importance, traditional differences have become more important again.

The PRC government has reduced the salience of these divisions by its attempts to prevent Taiwan from declaring independence. It wishes to divide the Taiwanese by scaring off those who are not implacably in favour of an independent Taiwanese state and isolating those who are. In fact, the more the PRC government regards the Taiwanese differently from the way they are regarded by their own government in Taipei, the more it reminds them of the differences between Taiwan and the mainland. The initial response of the PRC authorities to the massacre of 24 Taiwanese tourists on Qiandao Lake in Zhejiang province in 1994, which was to try to cover everything up, caused a wave of popular indignation on Taiwan. By threatening to use force the mainland risks uniting the Taiwanese against itself in a demand for independence.

The attitudes of other countries towards the predicament of the Taiwanese will also contribute to what happens. As was stressed in earlier chapters, one of the factors that pushed people into contemplating independence was the treatment of Taiwanese citizens when travelling abroad. The lack of respect was regarded as humiliating, given Taiwan's achievements. Grievances both of individual Taiwanese tourists and of government representatives stationed abroad are still keenly felt.[1] If other countries ignore these grievances and continue to behave as they have in the past, they may also encourage the Taiwanese to press for independence in the belief that only then will they be treated fairly and equally. Thus neglect may lead to the opposite of what most other countries wish. A more welcoming attitude need not imply full official recognition.

If the collective identity of the inhabitants of Taiwan is defined primarily by contrast with the mainland, it also needs to be defined by reference to the rest of the world. It is important for Taiwan to form an accurate picture of its place in the world, for otherwise it may embark on a course of action based on a miscalculation of the global response to it. This is especially true where the issue of independence is concerned.

However much the international community may be sympathetic to Taiwan's aspirations for international representation, especially at the UN, Taiwan's problem is that it is not important enough for other countries. It may be the twentieth largest economy in the world, with a per capita income approaching that of the poorer states of Western Europe and a population larger than those of three-quarters of the states represented at the UN, but its economy is still only slightly larger than that of Belgium and just over half that of the Netherlands. This makes it important but not vital to more developed nations. The latter are involved in the management of global affairs and on various issues cooperation with the PRC is necessary to make that task easier. Thus any declaration of independence by the people of Taiwan would be unlikely to elicit outside military support, although there would be considerable moral support. Taiwan is not big enough on its own to make an impact even on

Asia's political stage, let alone the world's. Unlike the PRC, it cannot make other nations take notice simply because it is there. So it needs to devise a role or series of roles for itself which will catch the attention of other states and win sympathy by demonstrating that it can make a positive contribution to the international political environment.

Above all, Taiwan needs to improve its relations with other states in East Asia. Metaphorically speaking, Taiwan is perched on the rim of Pacific Asia more than any other state in the region. It no longer has diplomatic ties with any state there. It needs to define for itself a role in the region, encouraging other states to take an active interest in its plight, which will presuppose a national identity located, in a spirit of cooperation with neighbours, in Asia.

To some extent the government has already begun to articulate such a role with its 'southwards diplomacy'. The economic underpinning of such a role is also being laid, as Taiwanese companies begin to do more business in the region: roughly half of all Taiwan's exports now go to Pacific Asia.

One other obvious channel for Taiwan's diplomatic activity is APEC, since Taiwan does have a seat there. As a multilateral organization promoting economic cooperation throughout the Asia-Pacific region, its goals are at one with those of Taiwan as a major trading nation. In so far as security problems of the region may be discussed at the margins of its summit meetings, APEC also can address one of Taiwan's security needs, namely a general discouragement of the use of force to solve international disputes, in particular by the PRC *vis-à-vis* Taiwan. It is true that Taiwan labours under a disadvantage there, in that other members of the organization have so far bowed to pressure from Peking and prevented President Lee Teng-hui from attending the summits in person. President Lee himself admitted in May 1992: 'We are all well aware that our capacity to contribute to Asian-Pacific regional linkage is limited.' He went on to urge the USA and Japan to take a lead in discouraging trade protectionism in the region.[2]

Yet Taiwan, too, should make every effort to encourage the strengthening of APEC and to make its own contribution to the organization. After all, it is sometimes smaller countries that play a greater role in developing transnational integration, for by so doing they enhance their own capabilities *vis-à-vis* larger and more powerful neighbours. This could be a national goal that would raise Taiwan's international profile in the region most important to it.

In some ways the status quo in relations between Taiwan and the PRC still has its attractions. Despite all the adversities, Taiwan has managed to turn the handicaps to its advantage, even when most isolated internationally, as in the 1980s. And certainly states in other parts of the world have also benefited from this status quo and are interested in trying to preserve it. There is no prospect of reunification.[3] Yet in the 1990s the status quo is more fragile than ever before, as factors that could disturb it have grown stronger on both sides of the Taiwan Straits. That is why it is impossible to answer definitively the question posed at the beginning of this book: will Taiwan try to 'take off' from the rest of China politically?

Ideally the leaders on both sides should engage in serious contacts and talks, if not to resolve the disputes, then at least to ensure that the situation does not get out of hand. However, Presidents Jiang Zemin and Lee Teng-hui are under considerable domestic pressure to assert their respective positions and not to make concessions – Jiang Zemin from the PLA high command, and Lee Teng-hui from the DPP. Serious political contact between them could in itself be construed by some of their opponents as weakness. Unless and until leaderships emerge on both sides of the Straits that feel self-confident enough to engage in serious talks, the situation will remain fragile.

Unfortunately much depends on the development of the political system on the mainland, and any precise prediction about its evolution is impossible. In the meantime, the developing democratic system on Taiwan gives people there the opportunity to make a vital contribution to the outcome, for how they vote in forthcoming parliamentary and presidential elections will determine the strength of President Lee Teng-hui's own position. All democratic systems have to balance rights and responsibilities. New democracies have to learn how to do this through practice. It cannot be taught. The trouble is that Taiwan has to learn this particularly quickly. In few states are the potential international consequences of getting it wrong so catastrophic.

Notes

1 For an outline of the difficulties faced by officials of the Taipei Representative Office in London, see Foreign Affairs Committee of the House of Commons (Session 1993–4, First Report), *Relations between the United Kingdom and China in the Period up to and beyond 1997* (London: HMSO, 1994), ii, pp. 358–9.

2 Lee Teng-hui, *Creating the Future* (Taipei, 1992), p. 143.

3 Jean-Pierre Cabestan, *Taiwan Chine populaire: l'impossible réunification* (Paris: Dunod for IFRI, 1995).